The American Assembly, *Columbia University*

OMBUDSMEN FOR
AMERICAN GOVERNMENT?

Prentice-Hall, Inc., *Englewood Cliffs, N. J.*

A SPECTRUM BOOK

LF

JK
468
O6
O5
copy 3

Preface

The Thirty-second American Assembly, at Arden House, Harriman, New York, October 26-29, 1967, described the Ombudsman as "an independent, high-level officer who receives complaints, who pursues inquiries into the matters involved, and who makes recommendations for suitable action. He may also investigate on his own motion. He makes periodic public reports. His remedial weapons are persuasion, criticism and publicity. He cannot as a matter of law reverse administrative action."

After discussion in depth the participants in the Assembly—including legislators, scholars, officials, and public affairs experts—acting in their private capacities approved a Final Report of findings and policy recommendations on the Ombudsman, stating that "there is a need in today's large and complex government for mechanisms devoted solely to receiving, examining, and channeling citizens' complaints, and securing expeditious and impartial redress." The Report may be had from The American Assembly.

This volume was prepared, under the editorial supervision of Professor Stanley V. Anderson of the University of California at Santa Barbara, as background reading for the Arden House Assembly. It is also intended for other meetings on this subject as well as for the student and general reader.

The opinions in the chapters which follow are those of the individual authors and not of The American Assembly, a non-partisan institution which takes no position on matters it presents for public discussion. Nor is The Ford Foundation, whose generosity made possible the entire Assembly program on The Ombudsman, to be associated with the views herein.

Clifford C. Nelson
President
The American Assembly

Table of Contents

The Problem of the Ombudsman's Compatibility with American Political Principles and Institutions, 63; Problems of American Culture, 66; Problems of Opposition to Adoption, 67; Problems of the Formative Years, 69.

Stanley V. Anderson

Introduction

Business agent, creditor's agent, insurance agent, local agent, press agent, sales agent, trade union agent: these are all "ombudsmen" in Swedish. Gullberg's Swedish-English dictionary uses four column inches to amplify the basic meaning of *ombud*: "representative, agent, attorney, solicitor, deputy, proxy, delegate." *Ombudsman* requires another couple of inches. Lawyers are ombudsmen, diplomats are ombudsmen, even members of Parliament are ombudsmen.

The Ombudsman whose origins are described in the first chapter of this book is *Riksdagens Justitieombudsman*, literally, "The Parliament's Agent of Justice," which sometimes gains in translation as "Parliamentary Commissioner for Civil and Judicial Administration." Happily, this lengthy title has been reduced to the initials "J.O." When the JO's jurisdiction over military administration was split off in 1919, *Riksdagens Militieombudsman*, "The Parliament's Agent for Military Affairs," took the popular designation of "M.O."

The third member of this triumvirate of initials is "J.K.," the *Justitiekansler*, or Chancellor of Justice. Before the Napoleonic wars

STANLEY V. ANDERSON is Associate Professor of Political Science at the University of California, Santa Barbara. He holds degrees in Philosophy, Law, and Political Science from the University of California, Berkeley, and a Certificate of Advanced Study from the University of Copenhagen. As Legislative Intern and Congressional Fellow, Dr. Anderson served with the California Assembly Committees on Judiciary and Constitutional Amendments and the United States Senate Judiciary Subcommittee on Constitutional Rights. As a practicing attorney he has been Assistant Public Defender in Alameda County, California. He has written widely on Scandinavian public law, including the institution of Ombudsman.

—when Finland was an integral part of Sweden—the JK was known as the Realm's highest deputy, *högste ombudsman,* a designation which is still accorded him in the Swedish Constitution.

Swedish is an official language in Finland, spoken as a native tongue by seven to eight per cent of the population, and as a second tongue by others. The jurisdiction of the Finnish JO (Finnish: *oikeusasiamiehen*) includes the military, and there is no separate MO in that country.

When the office of MO was adapted in Norway in 1952, and when provision for a JO was included in the 1953 Danish Constitution, the word ombudsman (Danish: *ombudsmand;* Norwegian: *ombudsmann* or *ombodsmann*) had to be restored. Particularly in Danish, the term had almost completely withered, being used only in phrases such as *borgerligt ombud,* that is, "civic duty," referring to the obligations of citizenship such as service on a jury.

In Denmark today, then, when one refers to the "Ombudsman," one has in mind the Parliamentary Commissioner, *Folketingets ombudsmand.* As in New Zealand, he is the only Ombudsman in the country. In Norway, one must distinguish between *Ombudsmannen for forsvaret,* "the Ombudsman for Defense," and *Ombudsmannen for forvaltningen,* "the Ombudsman for Administration," sometimes also called *Sivilombudsmann,* or "Ombudsman for Civil Affairs."

In Chapter 1, Professor Donald Rowat traces the diffusion of the term, the concept and the institution of Ombudsman around the globe. Clearly, the meaning which has been received into English is a narrow one, as in Danish. This, for example, is the definition found in those English dictionaries which have picked up the term, and in the *Encyclopaedia Brittannica* (1968 ed.).

There is a tendency, as Professor Rowat notes, for the specific signification to blur. Strictly speaking, the word "ombudsman" should be used in English only within the range of meaning which he carefully defines. It may be, however, that we will follow the Swedish example, and develop a vast array of ombudsmen. If so, we should follow the advice in the first chapter, and distinguish other applications—as the Swedes do—by the use of modifiers: campus ombudsmen, corporate ombudsmen, etc.

Of course, it is not the name but the need which has encouraged the spread. A good JO by any other name would still be wanted to humanize the remoteness and occasional harshness of the governmental side of our vast and complex modern society. But will this particular institution take hold in the United States, or will the American body politic resist the transplant? In his 1932 doctoral dissertation at the University of California (Berkeley), *The Development of Parliamentary Government in Sweden,* Professor Eric C. Bellquist includes a chapter on "The Riksdag as an Organ of Control." The JO is but one of ten parliamentary institutions (e.g., legislative auditors and supervisory committees) or procedures (e.g., interpellation and debate) described by Professor Bellquist for the control of government. First, this inventory reveals that the Ombudsman is not a panacea, even in its birthplace. Second, it is an indication of the need for caution in attempting transplantation. How does one determine whether an institution can be transferred, and, if so, with what appropriate changes?

Professor William Gwyn makes a seminal contribution to such investigation in Chapter 2. For the first time, the office of Ombudsman is defined not simply in terms of its Scandinavian characteristics, or those of New Zealand, but in terms of the favorable and unfavorable consequences we might expect of it here. Professor Gwyn goes on to consider whether present mechanisms—internal review, grand juries, intervention by legislators, etc.—meet the goals set for an Ombudsman.

One of these possibly alternative devices, the legislator as Ombudsman, is taken up for intensive scrutiny in Chapter 3. "If legislators are already doing the job, then we don't need an Ombudsman," one hears frequently from some opponents of the idea. Professor John Moore draws upon presently available information to try to tell us whether the lawmaker is doing the Ombudsman's job, and, if not, whether he might be able to do it. Professor Moore's answer is a plea for more data. This chapter and the preceding one map the frontiers of our present knowledge of American public complaint handling procedures, and reveal that exploration has just begun. Five years, ten books, fifteen theses, and twenty articles from now, we should know a great deal more.

Ironically, then, the greater difficulty in assessing the need for and potential success of Ombudsmen in American lies not in lack of understanding of the Ombudsman institution, but in scanty knowledge of related American institutions. Until this gap is bridged, we must rely upon implementation of Ombudsmen in the United States to provide tests of its efficacy. Professors Milton Kaplan and William Angus supply two extensive examples of American Ombudsmen in Chapter 4. One is an Executive Ombudsman (to use Professor Rowat's terminology), the Nassau County Public Protector. The other is a simulated Ombudsman, the Buffalo Citizens Administrative Service. Judging from their infancy, these offices seem to reveal a need and to fill it.

A more seasoned and clearly successful limited Ombudsman, the California Commission on Judicial Qualifications, is presented in Chapter 5, which also puts the substance of previous chapters into the mill of politics, using the California Ombudsman proposal as example. Scholarly analysis is the grist of that mill, and publicity the yeast. If the loaf rises when baked in the legislative ovens, then the process of legitimization is initially successful. The author predicts that sheer numbers will eventually bring the enactment of some Ombudsman proposals, and that these will encourage others.

Professor Rowat notes the traditional tie of the Ombudsman to the legislative branch, but emphasizes his independence. Professor Gwyn builds upon independence to argue that an exclusive legislative link is not essential. In the annotated statute which concludes this volume, Professor Walter Gellhorn urges that executive appointment with bicameral legislative confirmation would help ensure the consensus which would buttress that independence. This analysis is mirrored in the position taken by Republican Governor David F. Cargo of New Mexico, who stated "I wanted it, but I'm not very excited about having the Ombudsman appointed by the Legislature. I think this should be a joint [appointment] of the executive and the Legislature." [1] As another step in this progression of argument, perhaps it would be sufficient if the chief executive participated in the initial appointment of a particular Ombudsman, but not in his subsequent reappointment. Finally, Mr. Gwyn points out that the independence of the Ombudsman will increase with the length of his term.

In the Buffalo experiment which they supervise, Professors Kaplan and Angus have made a significant discovery. From their experience, a municipal and perhaps even neighborhood Ombudsman can handle complaints of local impact arising from governmental activity at the county, state or Federal level. The converse is probably not true, and so the Ombudsman is like the proverbial umbrella which can go up the chimney down but not down the chimney up. To accomodate overlapping jurisdiction, joint appointment of a regional Ombudsman is suggested.

Another solution would be for Federal, state and county legislative bodies to enact enabling legislation, giving local Ombudsmen jurisdiction over agencies within their respective spheres, when the complainant is local. If there are also Ombudsmen in these other spheres, no Ombudsman should take up a complaint which is under reasonably brief consideration by another appropriate Ombudsman. Under such legislation, county, state and national officials would be obliged to respond to inquiries from local or regional Ombudsmen, and to explain action taken, if any, in response to ombudsmanic recommendation. Obviously, such a fluid system can work only because the

[1] "Ombudsman Defeated in Close Senate Vote," *Albuquerque Journal*, March 8, 1967. The legislative history of the New Mexico Ombudsman proposal is sketched in Chapter 5.

Ombudsman has no power to change decisions, but has authority only to investigate and recommend. Enabling legislation might also be supplemented by grants-in-aid, setting standards of impartiality and expertise for the recipient Ombudsman office.

Let us conclude this prologue with a nutshell summary. Professor Rowat tells us what is being done elsewhere. Professor Gwyn analyzes what we might expect here. Professor Moore demonstrates that other mechanisms are not meeting these expectations. Professors Angus and Kaplan show how American approaches to Ombudsman do meet them in two places. For the rest of the country, Professor Anderson explains, help is on the way. Finally, Professor Gellhorn describes a specific form which that help might take.

Donald C. Rowat

1

The Spread of the Ombudsman Idea

In 1955 only three Scandinavian countries—Sweden, Finland and Denmark—had an Ombudsman system. In 1962 two more countries —Norway and New Zealand—adopted the plan. Since then the scheme has been adopted in five other countries around the world: Guyana, Mauritius, the United Kingdom, the Canadian provinces of Alberta and New Brunswick, and the American state of Hawaii. In addition, West Germany set up an Ombudsman for the armed forces in 1957, and the State Comptroller in Israel has assumed the complaint-handling function of an Ombudsman. By mid-1967, then, variations of the Ombudsman system existed in twelve countries. Not only that, but the scheme has been officially proposed or is being actively discussed in many other places around the world.

Why has the Ombudsman idea spread so rapidly in recent years? A short answer is that the growth of the welfare state has made necessary new protections against bureaucratic mistakes and abuses of power. The Ombudsman is a novel and uniquely appropriate institution for dealing with the average citizen's complaints about unfair administrative action. It differs from our traditional methods of

DONALD C. ROWAT *is Professor of Political Science at Carleton University, Ottawa, Canada. He has taught political science in the United States and Canada for many years, and served as a consultant on public administration for the United Nations in Ethiopia. He studied the governments of Western Europe, including the Ombudsman system in Scandinavia and the Conseil d'Etat in France. Professor Rowat has written several books on public administration, the latest being* The Ombudsman: Citizen's Defender.

dealing with grievances and has important advantages over these methods.

What is the nature of the original Ombudsman system? What changes were made when the scheme was transferred to other countries? What advantages does it have over other agencies here and elsewhere? Finally, what conclusions may be drawn regarding the application of the Ombudsman idea to the United States? These are some of the questions to be explored in this chapter.

Origins and Nature in Sweden and Finland

Though the Ombudsman plan is new in the sense that it helps to meet the problem of an expanded bureaucracy in the modern welfare state, it is actually an old institution in Sweden. The Justitie-ombudsman (JO) was first appointed as an officer of the legislature under the Constitution of 1809. His functions of receiving complaints from the people and protecting them against injustice were performed even before that date by an officer appointed by the King—the Chancellor of Justice (JK). When the legislature reasserted its independence from the executive in 1809, it decided to appoint the JO as its own "defender of the law." While the JK still exists and continues to receive complaints directly from the public, he has other important administrative duties, and the JO has become by far the more important officer for receiving and investigating complaints.

In the 19th century, the Ombudsman's activities were mainly concerned with supervising the courts and the police. The growth of administration in the 20th century has shifted his emphasis to the bureaucracy. In 1915 his docket became so heavy that a separate Ombudsman, the *Militieombudsman* (MO), was appointed for the armed services. Further growth in the work load has resulted in a recent proposal that an additional Ombudsman be appointed.

The origin of the Ombudsman in Finland is similar to that in Sweden. This is not surprising because for about six hundred years Finland was part of Sweden and had the same judicial and governmental system. Finland came under Czarist rule in 1809 and at the end of the century had a bitter experience with Russian attempts at oppression. So the Constitution Act of 1919, which created Finland as an independent republic, included institutions designed to protect the citizens against the arbitrary rule of officials. An officer similar to the Swedish Chancellor of Justice had existed in Finland since 1809, but he had in fact become much more important and powerful because he was regarded as a protector of the constitution and a bulwark aganist Russian domination. This office was continued under the Constitution of 1919, and the office of Ombudsman, modelled on the Swedish counterpart, was also created. Because of the traditional importance and power of the Chancellor of Justice in Finland, and his independence from the executive, he continues to be regarded as the chief defender of the law. Thus, Finland's basic law provides for two powerful and independent tribunes, one an arm of the executive side of government, and the other an arm of the legislature.

The Chancellor and the Ombudsman in Finland both have the power to prosecute not only the highest judges in the land but also government Ministers, and have upon occasion found it necessary to do so. Their complaint-handling functions, however, necessarily overlap. In order to avoid duplication, it was provided, in 1933, that the Chancellor should hand over to the Ombudsman complaints from prisoners and soldiers. Since many complaints are in this category, much of the load of investigating minor complaints is removed from the Chancellor's shoulders and the Ombudsman's labors are correspondingly increased. The Chancellor, however, still tends to deal with the more serious cases. He handles about 1300 cases per year, compared with about 1200 for the Ombudsman, and a considerably higher proportion require remedial action—about 20 per cent of the total, compared with about five per cent for the Ombudsman. The relative importance of their offices varies somewhat according to the political circumstances and the relative strength of their personalities. It is quite possible, of course, for an irate citizen to complain first to one and then, if he does not find satisfaction, to the other. This sometimes happens. But the two officers very seldom review each other's cases, and no conflict has arisen.

NATURE OF OMBUDSMAN SYSTEM

The Ombudsman institutions in Sweden and Finland have a number of unusual features which, in combination, make them unique among grievance-handling, appeal and investigating bodies. First, the Ombudsman is an officer of the legislature and not of the executive. He is appointed by the legislature, is free to report back at any time, and places before it a published annual report which describes and comments on important cases.

Second, he is an impartial investigator and is politically independent, even of the legislature. His office is set up by the constitution and once he has begun the investigation of a case the legislators do not intervene. By tradition, all important political parties agree on his appointment. Although he is appointed for a four-year term, he is frequently reappointed for a second or third term.

Third, a significant limitation upon the Ombudsman's power is that, unlike the courts, he has no right to quash or reverse a decision and has no direct control over the courts or the administration. His main power is the right to investigate and get at the facts. His influence is based upon his objectivity, competence, superior knowledge and prestige. When these are unpersuasive, his main weapon to secure remedial action is publicity—through his reports to the legislature and through the press. He does, however, have the power to prosecute officials for illegal acts. Although this power is seldom used nowadays, the fact of its existence no doubt increases the Ombudsman's influence.

Fourth, he has power to investigate on his own initiative. He can inspect courts and administrative agencies and can take up cases based on reports in the press. Evidence of the importance of these powers is that many of his most important cases, requiring a prosecution or a change in administrative practice or law, arise in this way.

Fifth, his method of handling appeals against administrative decisions is—unlike that of the courts—direct, informal, speedy and cheap. All that is required to initiate an appeal is for the complainant to write a letter. As an added protection for the large number of inmates of state institutions now found in the modern welfare state, letters from inmates of prisons and mental hospitals must be sent to him unopened by the supervisory staff. No formal court-like hearings are held, and the Ombudsman's work is done almost entirely by mail. He requests and studies departmental documents and, if not satisfied that a complaint is unwarranted, requests a departmental explanation. If the explanation is unsatisfactory, he will reprimand the official and try to secure remedial action. Where necessary, he will also recommend changes in laws and regulations designed to remove injustices in their application. Because his method of handling grievances is so informal and simple, his budget and staff are small. In Finland he operates with only four or five professional assistants; in Sweden, with ten.

An important feature of the Ombudsman's office is that, because of the simple and cheap way in which complaints are handled, many minor complaints can be satisfied. Though important to the complainant, they would not be worth the cost of an elaborate court procedure. Many cases involve no more than explaining to the bewildered citizen the reasons for the decision of which he has complained, and warning the government office in question that in future it should give adequate reasons for its decisions. Other examples of minor grievances are complaints about getting no answer to an application, leisureliness in replying to mail, giving insufficient information on a right of appeal, and delay in making decisions. Nevertheless, some of the Ombudsman's most valuable work has been done on serious cases of illegality involving the liberty of the subject, such as the unjustifiable use of handcuffs, or the recording of telephone conversations by the police, or an assault by a nurse on a mental patient.

Some idea of the nature and extent of an Ombudsman's work may be obtained by considering the number and disposition of the cases dealt with by the civil and military Ombudsmen in Sweden. The MO handles about 650 cases a year. Most of these arise from his own investigations, and fewer than 100 are based on individual complaints. The JO, on the other hand, receives about 1200 complaints a year, and in addition initiates about 200 inquiries on his own. Of his total number of cases, between 15 and 20 per cent require some sort of remedial action, such as criticism, recommendation, discipline or prosecution.

SAMPLE CASES FROM SWEDEN

A better understanding of the cases with which an Ombudsman deals, and the way in which he handles them, may be gained by reviewing some specific investigations made by an Ombudsman, and noting the action which he took. Here are some important cases as presented by the Swedish JO, Mr. Alfred Bexelius, to a sub-committee of the American Senate in March 1966:

> *Supervision of police*—(i) [A] man who was a habitual drunkard had, when drunk, maltreated his wife, who had been unfaithful to him. The wife went to the police, and the police—since the police doctor had examined him—sent the man to a mental hospital where he was detained for eight months. Then he complained to me. When I examined the hospital records, I couldn't find reasons to believe that the man was mentally ill. Therefore, I wrote to the Central Board of Health—the highest medical society in Sweden—and asked for their opinion. They answered that there had not been sufficient reasons to detain the man in a mental hospital against his will. Of course, the man could and ought to have been taken to a home for habitual drunkards but there he would not have been detained for more than three or four months. I didn't find reasons for prosecuting the doctor, but I wrote to the Government and asked them to give the man compensation.
>
> (ii) In the summer of 1963, two young girls were killed in Stockholm within a few weeks of each other by a sexual murderer. During the investigation carried out after the first crime, but before the second one, several tips were received from the public charging a certain man who was also interrogated by the police without, however, being found out until after the second murder. Critical viewpoints on the investigation were brought out in the press. I therefore found it necessary to make an investigation, and two members of my staff heard all the policemen who had worked on this case. On the basis of the findings of this investigation, I found cause for criticism of the work of the police. In particular, the number of persons taking part in the investigation had been too limited, and the system adopted for filing of the many items of information received from the public had not worked.

In this serious case, the Chief of Police should have more actively supervised the organization of the operation. It seemed all but incredible that the criminal had not been exposed earlier to prevent the second murder. The defects found in the work of the police in the course of this investigation led to the preparation of efficient plans for how the police were to operate in similar cases. This action proved to be of positive value for future work of the police in their duties to protect the general public.

*Administrators—Conflict of Interest—*In December 1961 the president of a private charter airline arranged a goodwill trip by air from Sweden to Paris called "The Christmas Shopping Trip." Through reports in the press I was informed about the fact that government officials had taken part in the trip. On my request, the matter was investigated. Participants in he trip were, *inter alia,* the Director of the Civil Aviation Inspectorate and his wife. Before the trip, the Director had submitted the question of his participation to his superior, the Director-General of the National Swedish Board of Civil Aviation, who gave him permission to take part in the trip. I found that the Director of the Civil Aviation Inspectorate had obviously been invited because of his official position. There was, though, no evidence of the assumption that he had allowed the exercise of his official duties to be influenced by the favor received. In view of the fact that his official duties covered inspecting and controlling functions against the company, he should not have accepted the invitation. By taking part in the trip with his wife, he had acted in a way which was likely to impair public confidence in the exercise of his official duties. By giving the other official permission to participate in the trip, the Director-General of the National Board of Civil Aviation had been neglectful of what, in the nature of his position, had been his duty in his capacity as head of the agency. The two officials were prosecuted and fines imposed. The decision was upheld by the Supreme Court of Sweden.

Judges and Courts—(i) A court had unjustly ordered an arrested person to pay the costs of his own return from the United States to Sweden for trial. The party complained to the Ombudsman on another aspect of the case. But, in his review, the Ombudsman discovered that the complainant had been wrongly made to pay his own transportation costs. Since the law was not clear in regard to the obligation to repay transportation costs, the judge could not be held responsible for the error. But the Ombudsman wrote to the Government and requested that the man be reimbursed. This request was granted.

(ii) The biggest enquiry which I have undertaken concerned the application by the courts of the laws on drunken driving. In Sweden it is an offence to drive a car if the alcohol content of the driver's blood is higher than 0.5 per mille at the time he is driving. In most cases, however, the blood test is taken some hours after the driving. This means that the courts have to estimate on the basis of the blood test how high the alcohol content was when the person was driving. In the courts this is called "calculating backwards." In the course of inspections, I noticed that when making these calculations the courts quite often started out from fallacious assumptions. In the scrutiny, the services of two prominent experts were used and with their aid it was shown how these "back calculations" ought to be made on a proper scientific basis. This enquiry, which was published in the annual report, has undoubtedly been useful to the courts.

The Graveyard Case—It happened a few years ago that a farmer was buried in a churchyard in the country. It was during the winter when the ground was covered with snow and it was difficult for the digger to find the family grave. A few weeks after the burial, the daughter of the farmer came to the rector of the parish and said that she was afraid that her father's coffin had been placed outside the family grave; and the rector went to the digger, but the digger said that he had not committed any fault; and then the daughter, who was a waitress, asked the municipal parish council for permission to investigate through digging, but the municipal council said "No."

Then she appealed in the ordinary way to the county board and there the governor of the county said "No." And so, she appealed to the Royal Cabinet. And the Minister concerned asked the Bishop and the Bishop said "No." And then the Cabinet said "No." Then she quarrelled with all the authorities concerned for many years, but they always said "No."

Then she complained to the Ombudsman. I sent that complaint to the municipal parish council and asked for information, but they didn't have much to say. Then I ordered the police to ask all persons who could give information. When I had got this information, I couldn't say with security if the coffin had been placed outside the family grave or not. But the circumstances were such that the parish council ought to have ordered an investigation through digging. The Ombudsman has no power to order digging in a churchyard. So, I couldn't do anything else than criticize the parish council because they had not made a real investigation in this case. But, the waitress took my decision and she went straight to the Cabinet Minister and said "Look here, Mr. Minister, here you see the Ombudsman says that there are reasons for investigation through digging," and so the Cabinet Council had nothing else to do than to order an investigation through digging. When they dug, they found that the coffin had been placed outside the family grave.

You can say that this case is a very small one, and it doesn't matter where that coffin was placed. But for the daughter, the case was of great importance, and even for all Swedes it is important to feel that they can get justice, even if the prestige of a Governor and a Bishop and a Cabinet Minister is involved.

This last case is perhaps more typical of the great bulk of cases with which the Ombudsman deals and the way in which he can secure remedial action on individual grievances. Many of them seem to be of little significance, yet are of great importance for the peace of mind of the complainant.

In summing up the nature of the Ombudsman's office, Mr. Bexelius stressed the following points:

One important aspect of the Ombudsman's activity which is often overlooked is the rejection of unwarranted complaints. Obviously it is of great interest to the official attacked that accusations of abuse are not left open, and that it is made evident by an impartial agency that the complaints were not justified. Also, it is of great importance that accusations made in the press regarding abuse by the authorities are taken up for investigation by an agency free of bureaucratic influence and that these investigations are available and the true facts made known to the general public. By the rejection of unwarranted complaints after proper investigation and on grounds clearly stated, the Ombudsman contributes to strengthening public confidence in the authorities and thus to a feeling of well-being in the society.

It should be emphasized that the office, by its mere existence, counteracts tendencies to transgressions of authority and abuse of powers. . . . The citizens have become increasingly dependent on public agencies. The need for a body independent of the bureaucracy for controlling the growing administration has therefore become more and more evident. . . .

It is . . . an expression for real democracy that the society keeps an institution with the task to protect the citizens against the society's own organs and that everybody in the society—even if he is poor and without social position—has the right to have his complaint against an authority investigated and tried by an impartial agency.[1]

First Adoptions Elsewhere

Considering the present world-wide interest in the Ombudsman idea, it is strange that the system was not taken up by any other country until after World War II. In 1952 Norway set up an Ombudsman scheme for the armed services. Denmark then made provision for a general Ombudsman plan under its new Constitution of 1953 and appointed its first Ombudsman in 1955. After that, the adoptions were more rapid. West Germany provided for a military Ombudsman in 1957, which is described in my symposium, *The Ombudsman.* Norway added an Ombudsman for civil affairs in 1962, and in the same year New Zealand became the first country in the Commonwealth to adopt the plan.

It is interesting to speculate on what had hindered and then furthered the international spread of this institution. It had functioned in Sweden since 1810. Why did Norway and Denmark not become interested in the scheme until after World War II, and why is it only now that the idea is being widely discussed in other democratic countries? The language, geographic position and cultural isolation of Finland and Sweden were no doubt significant barriers to the spread

---

[1] U. S. Congress, Senate, Committee on the Judiciary, Sub-Committee on Administrative Practice and Procedure, *Ombudsman* (March 7, 1966), 11-12. The cases cited are found at pp. 7-16 and 33-36.

of knowledge about the scheme, but these barriers did not exist for Denmark and Norway. The idea for a military Ombudsman in West Germany was originally proposed by a member of the federal legislature who had spent some time in Sweden as a refugee from Hitler. Other West Germans became interested because of their concern to create a democratic citizens' army. Probably the reasons a civil Ombudsman has not been seriously considered there until recently are because of Germany's well-developed system of administrative courts and because the office of military Ombudsman has not been a notable success.

The discussion of the idea in the English-speaking world and its adoption in New Zealand owe much to the ability of the first Danish Ombudsman, Prof. Stephan Hurwitz, to write and speak in English about his new office, and to his proselytizing zeal in doing so. He prepared a pamphlet in English, and wrote several articles for English periodicals and one for a law journal in the United States. He also spoke to academic audiences in Britain and appeared there on television. This no doubt stimulated much interest in Britain. In fact, after his return to Denmark he began receiving complaints against British administration! In 1959, a paper of his was read to a United Nations seminar in Kandy, Ceylon, which was attended by the Attorney General of New Zealand and by the Permanent Secretary for Justice. The idea for the scheme in New Zealand was stimulated by this meeting, as well as by early discussions in certain British periodicals, such as *Public Law*.

Geographic isolation and language may have been somewhat a barrier to the earlier adoption of the system outside Scandinavia, but these obstacles would not have been sufficient if social conditions elsewhere had called for it. This, I think, explains why Denmark and Norway, though having close linguistic and cultural ties with Sweden and Finland, did not adopt the institution until after World War II, and also explains the peculiar circumstance that Norway and far-away New Zealand created the system in the same year. With the expansion of state activity during and after the war, social conditions had become ripe for the adoption of the Ombudsman plan.

NATURE OF TRANSPLANTED PLANS

The comprehensive Ombudsman plans adopted in Denmark, Norway and New Zealand are modelled closely on the Swedish and Finnish originals. Although in most essentials they are the same as the originals, some signficant changes were made. It is mainly the new versions, especially the one in Denmark, which have become the model for the rest of the world.

Perhaps the most significant change was that, in all three countries, the Ombudsman was not given the power to supervise judges. This was partly because Denmark and Norway had no close counterpart of the Chancellor of Justice, and no tradition of his supervision over the courts. A second reason was that in these countries adequate supervisory machinery already existed within the court system itself. A third reason was the view that an agency of the legislature should not supervise the courts. This conventional wisdom has also prevailed in New Zealand, and, so far, elsewhere. Yet its logic is difficult to see. In Sweden the Ombudsman is non-partisan and independent of legislative influence in individual cases. He reviews judicial behavior, not the content of decisions, and he does not infringe on the political independence of judges. The Swedish Ombudsman has provided numerous examples which demonstrate that judges are only human and therefore fallible. The experience of the Commission on Judicial Qualifications in California, discussed in Chapter 5, bears out this conclusion.

A second important difference from the original systems is the confidentiality of the Ombudsman's investigations in all three countries. None of them has adopted the Swedish-Finnish principle that administrative documents are open to the public and the press. The amount of publicity given to a case is therefore mainly at the discretion of the Ombudsman himself, and ordinarily no publicity is given until an investigation has been completed. Since the publication of accusations against officials before verification by the Ombudsman is of dubious value, this change is probably desirable, unless the whole Finnish-Swedish system of general administrative openness is adopted, in order to implement the overriding principle of the public's "right to know" in a democracy.[2]

A third significant difference in the newer schemes is that the Ombudsmen have not been given the specific power to inspect or audit administrative transactions. As a result, they initiate very few cases on their own. In Sweden, on the other hand, a large proportion of the more serious cases arise in this way, and the Ombudsmen's recommendations on them result in important administrative improvements. The Swedish Ombudsmen thus act as permanent "Hoover" commissions on administrative procedure and efficiency. This is the main reason why 15 to 20 per cent of the civil Ombudsman's cases result in remedial action, compared with only 10 per cent or less for the newer plans.

Other differences are that in the newer plans the Ombudsman was not given the power to prosecute officials, and that in Denmark and

---

[2] See my "The Problem of Administrative Secrecy," *International Review of Administrative Sciences*, 2 (1966), 99-106.

Norway he was not permitted to criticize the wisdom or content of an administrative decision but only the fairness of the procedure by which the decision was made. These differences are not of great significance, however. In the newer schemes he may still order or recommend a prosecution. In the older ones and in New Zealand, the Ombudsmen rarely criticize the substance of decisions because they realize that in such matters they should not substitute their judgment for that of the responsible administrators. Since the line between the content of a decision and the way in which it is made is a thin one, the Danes have wisely given the Ombudsman a chance to intervene if necessary, by using a vague word to restrict his powers. He may challenge a decision if he thinks it "unreasonable." The Norwegian law restricts his powers a little more by saying that the decision must be "clearly unreasonable." New Zealand's law, on the other hand, may have gone too far in the other direction, by allowing him to intervene if he thinks a decision is "wrong."

THE PLANS IN OPERATION

The transplanted versions of the Ombudsman system seem to have worked with great success. Before adoption, especially in Denmark, the civil servants opposed the plan because they feared harassment by the Ombudsman and the attendant publicity. Afterward, however, they rapidly changed their views because they found that the Ombudsman's rejection of unwarranted complaints enhanced the public's confidence in the civil service. They even found the Ombudsman to be a valuable protection in their own complaints against superiors! Highly respected lawyers with much administrative familiarity were appointed as the first Ombudsmen, and they have been successively reappointed at the end of their four-year terms.

Case experience with the transplanted systems has been surprisingly similar to that in Finland and Sweden. In proportion to population, the number and types of complaints received (excepting, of course, complaints against the courts), and the number requiring remedial action, are roughly the same. All three countries have populations under five million, and each Ombudsman receives about 1,000 complaints per year. About a third of them are outside his jurisdiction and most of the remainder he finds unwarranted; but in up to 10 per cent of the total received, he finds that the complaint is justified and takes appropriate action to satisfy the grievance and improve the future efficiency of administration. Thus in the year ending March 31, 1967, New Zealand's Ombudsman handled 799 complaints, of which 444 were actually investigated. Of the 351 in which the investigation had been completed, 56 required remedial action.

SAMPLE CASES FROM NEW ZEALAND

In order to give the reader an impression of how the Ombudsman operates in a country which inherited the English parliamentary system and common law, some typical cases are presented below. These are taken from the annual reports of New Zealand's Ombudsman for the years ending March 31, 1966 and 1967. About 100 cases, involving more than 30 departments and agencies, were reported on each year. Most of them strike a familiar chord in the sense that they could easily have happened here.

Supervision of Police—Case No. 2054: The complainants in this case were father and son. The father held a responsible position in the community and expressed his concern regarding the manner in which his 22-year-old son had been questioned by a constable. In particular he objected to certain remarks which the constable had addressed to his son, and to the fact that the interrogation was carried out in an open office where a civilian staff member of the Police Department was working within earshot.

After studying the official files, I found that the Police had justifiable grounds for questioning the son in relation to certain conduct which had aroused the suspicions of the Police, but nevertheless the remarks made by the constable and the semi-public nature of the interrogation were both open to criticism.

On representing my views to the Department, it was agreed that some admonitory action would be taken.

I informed both complainants accordingly and subsequently received a letter of thanks from the father of the young man.

—Case No. 2336: The complainant's wife had her watch stolen by a young woman who was staying in the house and who was subsequently arrested on another charge. She denied stealing the watch, which was found in her possession, stating she had picked it up in the street.

The complainant claimed the watch on behalf of his wife, but the Police, after extensive inquiries, decided that the watch belonged to another person who had produced evidence of losing a watch with two numbers identical to those on the watch which the complainant claimed as his wife's. The Police declined to recognise the complainant's claim and he came to me.

The Police reopened their inquiries and subsequently found that the numbers on the watch were "batch" numbers, and, although similar to those of the other watch reported missing, indicated only that both watches were manufactured in the same lot. This led to a further interview with the young woman, who had previously stated that she found the watch, and she admitted stealing it from the complainant's house.

The watch was then restored to its rightful owner.

Conflict of Interest—Case No. 1753: A professional photographer complained that the driver of a Government tourist car was taking advantage of the opportunities offered by the nature of his occupation to operate a secondary business as a professional photographer and vendor of scenic photographs and postcards and of souvenirs. The complainant claimed that this amounted to unfair competition damaging to her own interests. On inquiry it transpired that the complainant's husband was also a Government tourist car driver, and, as my investigation proceeded, the wife of the driver, who was the subject of the original complaint, also complained in turn of the commercial activities of the complainant's husband.

As a result of my investigation both drivers were required by the employing Department [Railways] to give identical undertakings to the effect that their commercial activities would cease, and a general instruction in similar terms was sent to all other tour drivers.

Unemployment Benefits—Case No. 2043: The complainant, who had become unemployed, alleged that officials in the local office of the Labour Department had failed properly to advise her in respect of her entitlement to unemployment benefit and as a result she had suffered financial hardship.

On taking the matter up with the Department I found that there had been some misunderstanding on both sides. This was ironed out and resulted in the Department of Labour agreeing to recommend to the Social Security Department that retrospective payment be made for the period of unemployment.

This was done and the Social Security Commission subsequently approved of a benefit being paid.

The complainant, on receipt of the approved benefit, again complained, this time alleging that the benefit was paid only for a portion of the period of her unemployment, and I explained to her that a benefit is not normally granted in respect of the first seven days of a period of unemployment, and that such a period is deemed to commence after the date on which the payment of wages (including holiday pay) ceases.

Deportation of Aliens—Case No. 2365: The Minister of Immigration had issued a deportation order against an illegal immigrant who had married a New Zealand girl. The wife and her father made strong appeals, on personal hardship grounds, after representations to the Minister had been unsuccessful.

Because the order was lawfully made in accordance with firm Government policy by the Minister personally, the matter was outside my jurisdiction, and I could only suggest to the wife that if she were left in distressed circumstances as a result of the order, she should consult the local office of the Social Security Department.

Public Housing—Case No. 1866: This complaint related to the dilapidated condition of several departmental houses in a residential area. The complainant alleged that the disreputable state of the properties concerned had the effect of devaluing other properties in the locality.

The Department [of Railways] informed me that the houses had been purchased in connection with land acquisition for railway purposes and had not been specially acquired for staff housing. They were old and run-down when purchased and had there not been an acute shortage of housing would have been demolished. Most of the houses were let on a "restricted" tenancy basis, the occupants being responsible for maintenance.

Owing to the fact that the houses would have to be removed within a few years to make way for a new railway the Department felt that expenditure in renovation was not really warranted, but now agreed to do some minor repairs and external painting and to inform the tenants of their responsibilities in keeping the properties clean and tidy so that a reasonable standard of appearance would now be attained.

I informed the complainant accordingly.

Delayed Payment—Case No. 2554: The complainant had had difficulty in obtaining payment of a substantial amount of arrears of remuneration which he believed had been promised by the [Marine] Department. The amount was urgently needed to meet a family commitment. I asked the Head Office to look into the matter, and this resulted in arrangements for payment being made immediately.

Customs—Case No. 1736: The complainant was the father of a New Zealander serving at an overseas station of the Royal Air Force. In anticipation of leave in New Zealand in a few months' time, and of an expected reposting, the son sent several crates of his personal effects to his father, who was, however, informed by the Customs agents that the Customs would not permit him to collect the crates, and that in the meantime he would be required to pay 6s. per week storage.

The Customs Department explained that the agents had endeavoured to clear the crates under the tariff concession relating to passenger's baggage and effects, and in the meantime warehoused the goods pending the arrival of their owner.

As it was clear that the difficulties were due to lack of understanding and proper instructions as between the complainant, his son, and the Customs agent, the Collector of Customs at Auckland was asked to explain to the complainant precisely how the goods could be cleared (including the amount of deposit required against possible duty liability) pending his son's arrival. The complainant complied and secured delivery of the crates.

Voting Rights—Case No. 2930: An adult citizen of New Zealand had failed to enroll as an elector on attaining the age of 21 and was absent from his electorate during each of the next two Parliamentary elections.

He voted each time as an absentee voter, and did not become aware that his votes were invalid until he made inquiries in his own electorate after the rolls for the next election had closed. He then found that as he had never been on the roll, his previous votes must have been treated as invalid, and that he would not be able to vote in the current elections. He maintained that any voter whose vote was classed as invalid should be informed of the reason, so that he could correct the fault before the ensuing elections.

My inquiries showed that it was a normal and approved departmental practice for Registrars of Electors to take action to enroll those persons who had cast special votes but whose names did not appear on current electoral rolls. It seemed that the instructions on this point had not been followed on either of the occasions on which the complainant had cast a special vote. Accordingly the attention of all Returning Officers and Registrars was again especially drawn to the instructions by the Chief Electoral Officer, and the Department [of Justice] stated that consideration would be given to the desirability of amending the Electoral Regulations to provide that a special voter whose vote had been disallowed should be informed of the reason.

Public Employees—Case No. 1935: The complainant, who was over 65 years of age, had been employed on the temporary staff of the Public Service for almost 10 years. Although younger employees received 15 days leave after five years service, he was granted 10 days only and his application for 15 days had been declined.

When I took the matter up, the State Services Commission conceded that the complainant was entitled to 15 days leave under the existing legislation relating to annual leave, and I advised the complainant accordingly.

The case also drew to the Commission's attention a discrepancy between its Manual Instructions regarding annual leave and the legislative rulings under which those instructions were issued.

Postal Deliveries—Case No. 2629: A woman whose husband had left the family home complained that the Post Office was redirecting her mail to her husband under a redirection order which he had lodged with the Post Office.

On investigation I found that this had indeed occurred for a time as the Post Office had assumed that the whole family had shifted. However, on ascertaining the true position special steps had been taken to try to ensure correct delivery. Regrettably, a surprising number of letters continued to be wrongly addressed in one way or another—for example, letters to the wife having her initials but the prefix "Mr."—and this rendered the Post Office's task difficult. The Post Office also redirected to the husband any letters addressed to "Mr. and Mrs." jointly, and most of these were in respect of business matters for which the wife had become solely responsible after the separation.

Because of the continuation of such difficulties even after the complainant had shown that she had done all that she could be expected to do to secure the correct addressing of her correspondence, and because she had reason to believe that her estranged husband had not advised his correspondents of his change of address, she maintained that there should be a time limit on the operation of the redirection order, and also that mail jointly addressed should not be redirected.

I suggested to the Post Office that any letters addressed to the estranged husband and to him alone should be diverted from the home address where this appeared on the envelope, but the Director-General issued instructions that jointly addressed letters should continue to be redirected. He also stated that no special time limit would be put on the operation of the husband's redirection order or its renewal at the appropriate intervals if he were to apply. Although I was not happy with these decisions I doubted whether there were sufficient ethical or logical grounds for a formal recommendation on either point. I conveyed these views to the complainant and the Post Office.

The Post Office then sought the husband's cooperation in notifying all his correspondents of his change of address, and left open the possibility of a review of the position later. There was no doubt that the Post Office took special steps to try to be fair to both parties in a difficult situation.

What is striking in these cases is the role of the Ombudsman in humanizing administration. He accomplishes this by acting as a conduit of communication both between the citizen and goverment and among civil servants and departments. Not only are grievances remedied, but the likelihood of their reocurrence is lessened.

Recent Adoptions in Commonwealth Countries

One of the strongest early arguments against the Ombudsman was that the systems of government and law in Sweden and Finland were so distinct that the plan would not fit conditions in other countries. Its successful transfer to Denmark and Norway and especially to New Zealand, however, exploded this argument. New Zealand demonstrated that the plan could be successfully grafted onto the parliamentary system in a common-law country. On the other hand, all five of these countries were small in size and population, ranging from a population of well below three million in New Zealand to under eight million in Sweden. All five were also well-administered, developed democracies. There were therefore still doubts about how well it might work in populous, federal, racially heterogeneous, or developing countries.

Yet by the year 1967—only five years after the adoptions in Norway and New Zealand—the spread of the Ombudsman idea had gained such momentum that the plan had been adopted in five more countries: the United Kingdom, Guyana, Mauritius, the provinces of Alberta and New Brunswick in Canada and the state of Hawaii in the United States. By mid-1967, then, twelve Ombudsman plans were in existence: eight general plans at the national level, the specialized scheme for the armed services in West Germany, and the three plans for provincial or state governments in Canada and the United States. Except for Hawaii, the new adoptions were all in Commonwealth countries.

GUYANA, MAURITIUS AND CANADA

The first of the new adoptions were for Guyana and Mauritius, in 1965. Modelled on that of New Zealand, the plan was included in the new constitutions that these countries were to have when granted independence. Guyana gained independence in May 1966, and the

new Government, after consultation with the leader of the Opposition party, immediately appointed the former Director of Public Prosecutions as the Ombudsman. The effective date of the new constitution for Mauritius, and hence the appointment of an Ombudsman, was delayed until after the general election in the latter half of 1967. Both countries have a multi-racial population, and it was thought an Ombudsman would be valuable for protecting the rights of minorities against discrimination by officials.

In Guyana, the Ombudsman began his work slowly and his office was not widely known. He received only about 150 complaints during his first full year in office, and only one of these was an allegation of racial discrimination. Although there seems to be widespread agreement in Guyana on the need for such an office, it is too early to say how successfully it will meet the need. The work and effectiveness of the office will probably grow as it becomes better known.

In Canada, the legislature of Alberta provided for a provincial Ombudsman in March 1967. Earlier, the new post had been publicly advertised across Canada, and 232 applications had been received. In May the Government of Alberta announced that the new Ombudsman would be the retiring head of the Royal Canadian Mounted Police, George McClellan, who would take office in September. The legislature of New Brunswick also passed an Ombudsman Act in May 1967, and in October a former President of Mount Allison University, W. T. R. Flemington, was appointed as Ombudsman. The offices in both provinces are modelled on the New Zealand legislation. Canada's future experience with them should be instructive for state governments in the United States.

BRITAIN'S PARLIAMENTARY COMMISSIONER

The United Kingdom is the first populous country in the world to have created a general Ombudsman plan at the national level. Since Britain's democratic traditions and legal system are closely linked with those of the United States, the British scheme will be of considerable interest to Americans.

A detailed Ombudsman plan for Britain had been proposed as long ago as 1962 in a special report by the British section of the International Commission of Jurists, the so-called Whyatt Report. Although the idea was vigorously promoted, it was not accepted by the Conservative government. The Labour party, however, included the proposal in their campaign platform, and came into power in 1965 committed to its adoption. In the fall of 1965, the new Government published its proposals on the subject in a White Paper (Cmnd. 2767), but did not succeed in pushing a final version of its plan through both houses of Parliament until March 1967. Meanwhile, in July

1966, Prime Minister Wilson announced the appointment of the retiring Auditor-General, Sir Edmund Compton, to the new post of Parliamentary Commissioner for Administration. This appointment was greeted with consternation by many members of Parliament, not because of the person named, but because he had been appointed before the law creating his office had been approved by Parliament. Indeed, many thought it desirable that the retiring Auditor-General, who was already an independent officer of Parliament, should be appointed to the new post. Sir Edmund took office on April 1, 1967 with a staff of some 50 assistants, all drawn from the civil service.

The British scheme differs from the others in a number of important respects. Although the word "Ombudsman" is now part of the English language and is actually used in the legislation for the other Commonwealth plans, the British Government refused to use the word in its Act. Perhaps this is just as well, because the differences are so great that one hesitates to call it a genuine Ombudsman plan. These differences are based mainly on the conservative proposals of the Whyatt Report, which were designed to make the scheme more palatable to members of Parliament and to the Government.

The most radical difference is that citizens may not complain direct to the Parliamentary Commissioner. Instead, he must wait for complaints to be referred to him by members of Parliament, and he reports the results of his investigations to them rather than to the complainants. This provision was made partly through fear that an Ombudsman would short-circuit the relations between members of Parliament and their constituents, even though this has not been the experience in New Zealand. Accusations of maladministration and injustice make up only a small proportion of a legislator's dealings with his constituents. Because of their seriousness, these accusations should be handled differently from ordinary requests for favors. This change in the scheme deprives the citizens of two of the main advantages of the Ombudsman system—the complainant's right to appeal to a politically independent and impartial agency, and his right to be a direct party in his own case. It also prevents the Commissioner from investigating on his own initiative. Thus, he has been denied one of the Ombudsman's most important methods of discovering maladministration and improving efficiency .

A further serious limitation upon the Commissioner's powers is that a schedule to the Act gives a long list of matters which are not subject to his investigation. Among the most important of these are relations with foreign governments, security matters, police action, personnel matters in the civil service and the armed forces, public corporations, government contracts, regional hospital boards, the government of Northern Ireland, and local government. Whenever Ministers think it "in the public interest," they may instruct the Commissioner to refrain from the subsequent publication of documents and information obtained during an investigation. Also, he is debarred from matters for which there are remedies in the courts. Since Ministers can refuse to submit testimony to the courts, this provision has been criticized as intending to protect civil servants from embarrassing probings. Unlike the original Ombudsman scheme, the Commissioner is appointed by the executive rather than the legislature. However, he holds office during good behaviour and can be removed only by Parliament.

While the Bill was before Parliament, the Government itself moved an important amendment which would have provided that the Commissioner could not review by way of appeal any discretionary decision. This amendment was attacked on the ground that it would emasculate the Commissioner's powers altogether by making it impossible for him to investigate any of the thousands of decisons where administrative authorities have a discretion. The Government finally substituted another amendment which says that he may not question a discretionary decision "taken without maladministration." This is still a far cry from the provision in the New Zealand legislation which allows the Ombudsman to review a decision if he thinks it is simply "wrong."

Because the limitations placed upon the Commissioner's scope and powers were so great, the Government was subjected to much criticism by the Opposition and the press. The Commissioner was amusingly described as a "muzzled watchdog," a "crusader without a sword," and an "Ombudsmouse." It was even suggested that the date he took office, April 1st, was significant. Certainly, Britain seems to have adopted the plan in an unnecessarily truncated form. It is often argued regarding the proposal for an Ombudsman that his scope and power should be limited at first because it is a new experiment. Yet this very limitation may make the plan ineffective. Also, once an institution has been created, it is difficult to change. Hence there is a strong argument for granting the necessary scope and power from the beginning.

Recent Proposals Around the World

In recent years, the Ombudsman idea has spread to many democratic countries of the world. Partly responsible for this have been the activities of the International Commission of Jurists and the United Nations. Both have taken an active interest in the idea, and both have organized periodic conferences on human rights in various parts of the world, at which the idea has been discussed. These conferences have included key officials from most of the countries in the area concerned. The International Commission of Jurists has published frequent articles on the subject in its *Bulletin*. In 1965 its special British Guiana Commission of Inquiry on Racial Problems in the Public Service recommended the scheme, and was thus partly responsible for its adoption in the new constitution for Guyana. In 1966 the Jurists held a colloquium on the rule of law in Ceylon which reported favorably on the plan for the Asian and Pacific region. In 1967 the U.N. held a similar seminar in Jamaica for Central and South America, with the Swedish Ombudsman as a guest expert. The Latin American delegates concluded that the Ombudsman system would be desirable for their countries and that the U.N. should publicize it in Latin America. As a result of such world-wide discussions, Ombudsman proposals have been made not only in the United States and Canada, but also in Australia, several countries of Western Europe, and a number of developing countries.

CANADA AND AUSTRALIA

The Ombudsman has been discussed in *Canada* since 1961. (Professor Anderson gives a full account of the discussion in his *Canadian Ombudsman Proposals*). Besides the recent adoptions in Alberta and New Brunswick, the Governments of Manitoba and Quebec have committed themselves to introducing the plan, and it is being considered by a number of the other provinces. In the fall of 1966 the Government of Manitoba issued a White Paper, the *Citizen's Remedies Code*, which indicates that Manitoba may follow Britain in requiring complaints to be referred by members of the legislature. By mid-1967, however, the Governments of neither Manitoba nor Quebec had presented draft Bills to their legislatures, and it seemed unlikely that they would do so before 1968. At the local level, the mayor of Laval, the second largest city in Quebec, has declared that he favors an Ombudsman plan for the city, and an official commission has included the plan in its proposal for a metropolitan government across from Montreal's south shore. At the federal level, a committee of the House of Commons in 1965 recommended the scheme for the federal administration, and at that time Prime Minister Pearson announced that the idea would be referred to a new Royal Commission on administrative bodies. This Commission was not appointed, however, and no further action had been taken by mid-1967. Nevertheless, the recent adoptions in Britain, Alberta and New Brunswick will no doubt give a strong push toward further provincial adoptions and the creation of a scheme at the federal level in Canada.

The Ombudsman has also been discussed in *Australia* for several years. Because of Australia's federal system and close links with New Zealand, it seems strange that the plan has not yet been adopted there. It has been actively discussed by the press and politicians, however, and numerous proposals have been made, especially at the state level. In 1966, the Government of New South Wales referred the idea to a Law Reform Commission and requested a draft Bill. Although the federal Government has so far insisted that an Ombudsman is unnecessary, the plan may be adopted soon by one of the states.

WESTERN EUROPE

Because *Ireland* has close linguistic and cultural ties with the English-speaking world, there has been considerable discussion of the plan in that country. Although the Irish Government has so far taken the view that an Ombudsman is unnecessary, the idea is being considered by the Public Services Organization Review Group, recently set up by the Minister for Finance. The continental democracies, perhaps because they have more comprehensive systems for administrative appeal, have not taken as much interest in the Ombudsman as has the English-speaking world. Still, there has been considerable discussion in the Netherlands, Switzerland, Austria, and recently in West Germany.

In the *Netherlands,* following a study of the Scandinavian plan by J. G. Steenbeek, a commission of the Society for Administrative Law recommended it in 1964, and included a draft Bill in its report. This report was discussed at the Society's annual meeting in September 1964, and most of the speakers were in favor of the plan. Although the Government has taken no action on the proposal, in February 1967 the Committees for Petitions of both chambers of the legislature proposed that they should be given the same powers as a parliamentary commission of inquiry to inspect documents and hear public officials. They also recommended that an office should be set up to prepare the reports of the two committees.

The proposal has been discussed in *Switzerland* since 1960, when the Danish Ombudsman made a speech in Bern on the invitation of the Swiss Society for the Rule of Law and Individual Freedom. The chairman of the Society subsequently published a paper proposing that the system should be introduced by an amendment to the Swiss Constitution. In 1962 a commission of the Society proposed the appointment of both civil and military Ombudsmen. This proposal was widely discussed in the press. In 1964 a Swiss scholar, Dr. Walter Haller, produced a book in German on the Swedish Ombudsman. In the same year, Switzerland experienced its own version of the British Crichel Down Affair, and a special parliamentary Commission of Investigation had to be appointed. This has naturally enlivened the discussion of the subject.

In *Austria,* discussion appears to have begun with an article published in 1961. In 1963 the Danish Ombudsman made a speech in Vienna, and since then the idea has been repeatedly discussed. In *West Germany* serious discussion of an Ombudsman plan for civil affairs began about 1965. A society has been formed to support the idea, and unofficial Ombudsman proposals have now been made for the "city-states" of West Berlin, Bremen and Hamburg. The Hamburg proposal was in the form of a detailed draft bill modelled on the Danish plan, and was published in *Mensch und Staat* (no. 1, 1967), a journal of opinion which strongly supports the Ombudsman idea. In August 1967, Willi Weyer, Minister of Interior for North-Rhine Westphalia, the largest state in the federation, proposed the consideration of a civil Ombudsman plan by the permanent Interstate Conference of Ministers of Interior, and on September 1 one of the most widely-read weeklies, *Christ und Welt*, published an article entitled, "When Will a West German Ombudsman Come?" The federal Minister of Justice, Gustav Heinemann, favors an Ombudsman plan for civil affairs, but feels that it should be tried out first in one or two of the smaller states. Because Austria, Switzerland and West Germany are all federations, they have the advantage of being able to experiment with the plan at the state level.

DEVELOPING COUNTRIES

In additon to Guyana and Mauritius, the Ombudsman idea has been given an enthusiastic reception in a number of other developing countries. The plan has been seriously discussed in Malaysia, Jamaica, and Hong Kong, and official bodies have made detailed proposals for Singapore and India. In *Hong Kong*, the scheme was proposed by some of the elected members of the urban council in 1966, but the British governing authorities of this Crown Colony have so far refused to accept it. A committee of the Jamaican section of the International Commission of Jurists reported favorably on the plan in July 1967. In *Singapore*, a special Constitutional Commission headed by the Chief Justice was set up after Singapore's break with the Malaysian federation. In December 1966, this Commission recommended constitutional provisions for an Ombudsman very much like those for Guyana and Mauritius. The Government of Singapore has so far refused to adopt the plan on the ground that there has not been enough experience with it yet in other Commonwealth countries.

Of more relevance to American discussions is the recent proposal for *India*. India is a huge federal state, with a heterogenous population. Some of the problems of adjusting the plan to fit such a country are similar to those in the United States. The Ombudsman idea has been discussed in India for several years, and proposals have been made at both the state and federal levels. In 1963, the scheme was proposed by an official commission for the state of Rajasthan. Several other states have set up Ombudsman-like Vigilance Commissions to deal mainly with the problem of corruption. These commissions, however, are appointed by and responsible to the executive. Early in 1966 the Punjab Administrative Reforms Commission recommended that "in order to increase the utility of the Vigilance Commission, it should be made independent of government or ministerial influence."

At the federal level, a Committee on the Prevention of Corruption in 1964 rcommended the creation of a Central Vigilance Commission, to he headed by a single Commissioner and composed of three Directorates—Complaints and Redress, Vigilance, and Central Police. The Commissioner would be appointed for a six-year term and would have the same independence as the Auditor-General. His functions and powers would be somewhat like those of New Zealand's Ombudsman, except that he would also inspect for corruption and could initiate a prosecution against an official. The Government immediately created a Vigilance Commision, but its powers were limited, and the proposal for a Directorate of General Complaints and Redress was rejected. Instead, in January 1966 the Government appointed a Commissioner for Public Grievances in the Ministry of Home Affairs to handle complaints and supervise new departmental complaint officers. The Commissioner and departmental officers, however, are themselves part of the administration.

In October 1966, the Federal Administrative Reforms Commission, whose chairman a few months later became Deputy Prime Minister, published a special interim report proposing a new scheme for independent grievance officers. This scheme is unusual in that it would include both levels of government and at the same time divide the top from the lower levels of administration. There would be a sort of super-Ombudsman (the Lokpal) with jurisdiction over both federal and state Ministers and Secretaries. There would also be a lower order of Ombudsman (the Lokayukta), one for the federal government and one for each state, to cover the levels below the federal and state Secretaries. These officers would all be appointed by the President of India, would be answerable only to him and to the federal or state legislatures, and would be independent of the federal or state Cabinets. The Lokpal would be appointed on the advice of the Prime Minister, but only after he had consulted the Chief Justice and the leader of the Opposition. A state Lokayukta would be similarly appointed on the advice of the Chief Minister of a state. The Commission claims that the scheme could begin without a constitutional revision, but that eventually such a revision would be necessary.

In August 1967 the Government announced its acceptance in principle of the proposal for a Lokpal, but the states fear the supervision by the central government that such a scheme implies.

The developing nations in which the Ombudsman plan has been adopted or seriously proposed so far are Commonwealth countries which have inherited the British common law and a concern for protecting civil rights and controlling the executive. These countries have traditions akin to those in the United States. They also have similar, though admittedly more serious, problems of heterogeneous populations, political corruption and partisan influence in administration. Ombudsman proposals for these countries, and their experience with the plan, are therefore well worth studying. Although the need for an Ombudsman system in other developing countries is likely to be recognized, in the non-democratic ones the version adopted will no doubt be a weak office subjected to the control of the chief executive.

Related Institutions

Because the rise of the positive state in the twentieth century has resulted in a vast bureaucracy in most countries of the world, it is not surprising that a number of them have developed administrative complaint or appeal bodies similar to the Ombudsman institution. Some are more like it than others, of course. The main measures of their similarity are the degree to which they are independent of the executive and the extent to which they lack the power to make binding decisions. For instance, there is the Office of the Procurator in the Soviet Union and some other Communist countries, which is controlled by the executive and, in turn, has control powers over the administration. There are agencies like the Administrative Inspection Bureau in Japan, which are part of the executive but have mainly mediating or advisory powers. There are the administrative appeal courts in Western Europe, which are largely independent of the executive, but have the power to make binding judicial decisions. There are also the appointed legislative auditors, who as officers of Parliament are quite independent of the executive, but who rarely handle complaints from the public. In recent times, there have even developed purely private organizations which take up the cudgels for the wounded "little man" in his fight against the bureaucratic monster.

EXECUTIVE COMPLAINT AGENCIES

Of the special complaint-handling agencies set up as part of the executive branch of government, among the most interesting are those found in the Soviet Union, Japan, and the Philippines. The Inspector

General of the U.S. Army provides an American example of similar machinery at the federal level for handling complaints from soldiers.[3] Although these institutions do good work in investigating complaints and preventing maladministration, they lack the Ombudsman's essential characteristic of independence from the executive because he is an agent of the legislature.

There are many other examples of executive complaint bureaus around the world and at all levels of government. Those that exist in several American cities and states will be discussed in later chapters. Israel's two main cities, Jerusalem and Tel Aviv, have similar bureaus. The state Vigilance Commissions in India have already been mentioned. At the national level, Singapore has a special complaint bureau in the office of the Prime Minister. An interesting new example is the Permanent Commission of Inquiry in Tanzania. This body was set up in 1966 on the recommendation of Tanzania's One Party State Commission, and has been strongly influenced by the Ombudsman plan. It enquires into allegations of abuse of power by both public and party officials, receives complaints directly from the public, and has the power of access to government documents. The President appoints the three members for only two-year terms, the Commission reports only to him, and he has the power to stop any inquiry.

ADMINISTRATIVE APPEAL COURTS

Although there are many examples of administrative courts in the common-law countries, they are all for special purposes. In most areas of administration, there is still no right to appeal a decision to an independent body except to the ordinary courts on a question of law. In several countries of Western Europe, on the other hand, there are comprehensive administrative courts for the general appeal of decisions. These courts are separate from the regular courts and possess varying degrees of comprehensiveness and of independence from the executive. The most comprehensive and independent are found in France and West Germany. The French system, headed by the *Conseil d'Etat* (discussed in Chapter 2), is the most renowned for its independence from executive authority and for its protection of the individual against simple maladministration as well as abuse of power. An essential difference from the Ombudsman is that administrative courts have the power to quash or reverse administrative decisions.

In reviewing administrative action, administrative courts enjoy a number of advantages over ordinary courts. Among these are cheapness to the complainant, greater ease and informality in lodging a

[3] The institutions in Russia and Japan are described fully in Professor Gellhorn's *Ombudsmen and Others,* and those in the Philippines and the U. S. Army are discussed in *The Ombudsman.*

complaint, and the expertise of the judges in administrative matters. However, their transplantation to the common-law world would require a major revolution in our system of courts and administrative law. Furthermore, because they follow court-like procedures, they suffer—but of course to a lesser extent—from some of the disadvantages of the ordinary courts. Sweden has found it desirable to have both a Supreme Administrative Court and Ombudsman. Even in countries which have comprehensive administrative courts, then, an Ombudsman system might be a valuable addition to the machinery for controlling the administration.

LEGISLATIVE AUDITORS

Among related institutions, the legislative auditor is the closest parallel to the Ombudsman in that he is an independent officer appointed to investigate and report to the legislature on administrative action. Examples are the Auditors-General in Commonwealth countries, and the Comptroller-General in the United States. Ordinarily they conduct only a post-audit, and have no direct control over the administration. Although they specialize in financial transactions, it has been suggested that they could take on the functions of an Ombudsman by making general administrative inspections and investigating complaints from the public. Some of them have actually done so. In Canada, for instance, it was suggested in a broadcast on the Ombudsman idea that the public should send their administrative grievances to the Auditor-General. As a result, he received a considerable number of complaints by mail. He decided to send those that seemed warranted to the appropriate agency for an explanation, and through the influence of his office successfully secured remedial action in many cases.

The outstanding example of a legislative auditor who performs the Ombudsman function is the State Comptroller of Israel. His position and powers are much like those of an Ombudsman. Unlike most legislative auditors, he has a broad power to inspect for not only fiscal regularity but also administrative efficiency, propriety and ethics. Staffed by efficiency experts, his office is a sort of permanent commission on administrative organization. Unlike the American Comptroller-General, he has no direct power over the administration. He can only advise, criticize, and report to the legislature. From the outset in 1950, the State Comptroller considered it part of his job to investigate complaints from the public as an aid to his supervision of the administration. Although his complaint-handling function was not at first widely known, gradually it became more and more popular. Thus the number of complaints rose from 1300 in 1961 to 3100 in 1966.

Indeed, the Ombudsman idea has become so popular in Israel that a separate Ombudsman has been proposed. However the inspection function of the State Comptroller closely parallels that of the Swedish Ombudsman, and he has the added advantage of a large corps of experienced investigators. It is very likely, therefore, that the complaint-handling function will be left with the State Comptroller but will be highlighted by making specific legal provision for it.

Although in recent years the number of complaints and the State Comptroller's method of handling them have probably been influenced by the Ombudsman idea, Israel provides an interesting example of the independent development of an institution closely parallel to the Ombudsman. For legislative auditors in other countries to attempt the role of an Ombudsman would probably require a specific legislative mandate to broaden their supervisory powers and provide for the complaint-handling function.

PRIVATE ORGANIZATIONS

In many countries there are private welfare organizations and legal aid bureaus which are willing to take up the cases of helpless individuals who have been unjustly treated by administrative agencies. Some of those that exist in the United States will be described in later chapters. An interesting similar agency in Canada was an organization called "Underdog," which was founded in 1961 by a former newspaper man to help mistreated people. The founder began his operations simply by placing classified advertisements in city newspapers across Canada, offering to help mistreated "underdogs." As his number of cases grew, he enlisted the support of volunteer investigators in the cities from which the complaints came. He also assembled an advisory committee for difficult cases, and began expanding his activities and network of volunteer investigators to other countries. In 1962 the organization received over 1100 allegations of mistreatment. Although it handled any type of case, many were complaints against government administration and many of these were thought to be justified. At the author's request, the head of Underdog analyzed his Canadian complaints against official action and found that in the first eighteen months of operation Underdog had received 173 such complaints, of which 69 had to do with the federal government, 84 were provincial and 20 were municipal.

By 1964 Underdog had expanded its activities into fifteen countries, including the United States. It was only a shoestring organization, however, financed by volunteer contributions and help, and was primarily a one-man show. Its founder's chief weapon for obtaining remedial action was publicity. In fact, his methods for publicizing cases of alleged mistreatment were so unorthodox that they culminated in a spectacular incident in the fall of 1964. Wishing to publicize the plight of a man who claimed he was wrongly suspected of being a Communist because the Royal Canadian Mounted Police refused to acknowledge his activities as an undercover agent, the head of Underdog threw a milk carton of cow's blood on the floor of the House of Commons; he was promptly jailed, and became popularly known as the "Blood Bomber." This ridiculous publicity stunt ruined the future usefulness of the organization. Nevertheless, its rapid spread into many other countries is a good indication of the growing need everywhere for additional machinery to investigate individual complaints against both private and public administration.

A similar recent development has been the rapid growth of complaint columns in large daily papers, the so-called "newspaper Ombudsmen." By 1967 more than two dozen big dailies in the United States and several in Canada and Australia had such columns. Some have large staffs which handle hundreds of letters a week and thousands of telephone calls. The results of their action on complaints are often reported directly to the complainant and only a small portion actually appear in print. Although these columns handle any type of grievance, they play a role surprisingly like that of Ombudsmen when investigating complaints against official action. Their main disadvantage, however, is that they have no official power to get at government documents, inspect administrative activities, or influence the administration. Also, their coverage of the population is spotty, their budgets vary, and their staff's knowledge of administrative law is erratic. Nevertheless, the thousands of complaints against official action received each year demonstrate that the job of investigating them is too big for elected representatives to handle by themselves.

Further confirmation that legislators cannot do the whole job is the existence of similar private organizations in Britain which developed before the creation of the Parliamentary Commissioner. These are the Citizens' Advice Bureaux Service and the John Hilton Bureau. The former offers free information and advice to citizens, and comprises over 400 separate bureaus in nearly all the cities and many of the towns in the United Kingdom. These bureaus are staffed mainly by volunteers but usually have a panel of expert consultants on special subjects. Many of their cases involve administrative action. For serious cases they have a national committee which can deal with the central administration. The John Hilton Bureau is maintained by a national newspaper, and advises readers on social and personal problems. It has a staff of about 40, many of whom have professional qualifications, and it handles about 200,000 inquiries a year. Like the complaint columns, however, the emphasis of these two organizations is more on giving information and advice than on investigating allegations of maladministration or injustice.

Uniqueness of Ombudsman System

In the United States the Ombudsman idea has recently become so popular that the word "Ombudsman" is now being used to describe any new complaint-handling or appeal machinery. Thus, the term Tax Ombudsmen has been applied to a federal proposal by Senators Warren Magnuson and Edward V. Long to appoint administrative appeal court judges for small tax claims. The most serious misapplication of the term has been to complaint officers who are appointed by and responsible to the executive side of government. The Public Protector appointed in May 1966 by the Executive of Nassau County, for instance, as discussed in chapter four, is popularly called an Ombudsman. Similarly, several more recent provisions or proposals for executive complaint officers at the state and local levels have used the term. Unfortunately, this usage is likely to confuse the public and cause them to lose sight of the important point that the Ombudsman in other countries is an independent officer of the legislature.

Even in non-governmental organizations, new complaint officers are being set up called Ombudsmen. Thus the President of the State Bar of Michigan has appointed the seventeen Past Presidents as an "Ombudsman committtee" to hear complaints from members of the bar against its own officers. And, the State University of New York at Stony Brook has appointed faculty members as "Ombudsmen" to receive student appeals. Several other campuses, including the University of California at Berkeley, may do the same. The name *Ombudsman* has even been given to the person handling customers' problems in a San Francisco department store. Although the spread of the Ombudsman idea to private organizations is no doubt of value in promoting due process of law in private administration, the indiscriminate use of the word may rob it of its essential meaning.

It is perhaps already too late for the popular use of the term to be restricted to an officer responsible only to the legislature, as "JO" and "MO" are in Swedish. If so, writers who refer to other kinds of grievance officers should be careful to use an appropriate qualifying word—executive Ombudsman, university Ombudsman, newspaper Ombudsman, etc. In any case, every effort should be made to apply the term only to *politically independent* grievance officers. Otherwise, confusion is likely to prevail, and many American Ombudsmen will end up in the vest pockets of chief executives.

A comparison of the Ombudsman system with existing administrative complaint and appeal machinery in the English-speaking world and with related institutions elsewhere indicates that it is unique. Although many of the related institutions have some of its features, none of them—except possibly the State Comptroller in Israel—possesses the Ombudsman's unique combination of characteristics: *he is an independent and politically neutral officer of the legislature, usually provided for in the constitution, who receives and investigates complaints from the public against administrative action, and who has the power to criticize and publicize, but not to reverse, such action.* This unique combination means that the Ombudsman system is a new development in the machinery of democratic government as important as the invention and spread of the secret ballot or the public corporation. One can expect that it will continue to spread throughout the democratic world.

William B. Gwyn

2

Transferring the Ombudsman

One of the oldest branches of enquiry into politics is constitutionalism, the investigation of the means for creating and maintaining governmental systems which are at once efficient in their operations and safe for the governed. As an essay in constitutionalism, the present chapter attempts to answer two important questions regarding the introduction of the Ombudsman into the United States. First, is there a need for the institution in this country? Secondly, if there is a need, can the obstacles to its introduction be overcome?

Although the author believes that present knowledge suggests an affirmative answer to both questions he is well aware that we still do not know enough about the need for an Ombudsman in the United States or about its operations and effects abroad. The problem has not been one of an absence of writing on the Ombudsman for the bibliography on the subject is lengthy and growing. This literature, however, has frequently consisted of superficial formal descriptions of the office, similar to previously published descriptions and accompanied by little theoretical analysis or empirical research. The function served by such writing has been that of disseminating the idea of the Ombudsman throughout the world, but while this is important from the standpoint of the eventual spread of the institution it has done little to advance our understanding of it and of the circumstances in this country relevant to its adoption. The almost simultaneous publication of Professor Walter Gellhorn's two books *When Americans Complain* and *Ombudsmen and Others* has gone a long way toward remedying

WILLIAM B. GWYN, *Associate Professor of Political Science at Tulane University, has taught political science at the University of Tennessee and Bucknell University, and is the author of two books on government, including* The Meaning of the Separation of Powers.

our defective understanding, but much work remains to be done. It is the purpose of this essay to put forward an analysis of the problems of transferring the Ombudsman to the United States based upon current empirical knowledge. Even should later research prove the conclusions wrong, the framework of analysis may continue to be useful.

The Nature of the Ombudsman

To answer adequately the two questions raised in this chapter it is necessary to ascertain the structure (pattern of activities) of the Ombudsman, the desirable and undesirable consequences of that structure, and the environmental conditions which allow the institution to perform as it does. This task is complicated by the fact that we are concerned not with an actual institution existing historically but with a theoretical model refined from the historical experience of the five countries possessing operating Ombudsmen, as described in the preceding chapter. In analyzing the structure of the Ombudsman we are not concerned with all of the characteristics common to the five actual Ombudsmen but only with those which experience has shown to be necessary to accomplish the desirable consequences of the institution. From the standpoint of persons considering the adoption of an institution, its desirable consequences are regarded as achieving the goals of the institution. It is clear that any account of the structure and consequences of the Ombudsman is provisional and subject to revision in the light of further research and analysis. Additional knowledge about the operations of foreign Ombudsmen might force one to conclude that what was accepted as a desirable effect of the institution does not exist or only to such a small degree as to be trivial from the viewpoint of a nation considering adoption. Or one might discover further desirable consequences of the actual Ombudsmen, which might in turn draw our attention to the functional character of certain of their activities not included in the present model. Similarly, one might discover that aspects of the Ombudsmen's activities not previously recognized as contributing to goals included in the present model are in fact functional. Finally, it is possible that one might disclose further undesirable consequences resulting from the otherwise functional activities of the Ombudsmen, which might bring about a revision in the current assessment of the institution's utility.

STRUCTURE

The structure of the Ombudsman [1] would seem to be adequately

[1] The term "Ombudsman" is used throughout this paper to refer both to the official called by that name and the collective body composed of the official and his staff. The meaning should be clear from the context.

described by the following list of interrelated activities. Activities concerned with the impartial handling of individual complaints against particular administrative acts are generally seen as the institution's basic function. Thus a synonym for Ombudsman popular throughout the English-speaking world is "grievance-man" and even those who use other expressions such as "citizens' protector" or "citizen's defender" employ the handling of citizens' complaints as the defining characteristic of the institution. That the complaint procedure is viewed as basic in the countries having Ombudsmen is suggested by the fact that the size of the Ombudsman's staff is mainly determined by the load of complaints.

(1) The Ombudsman receives complaints from individuals who believe they have been mistreated in some way by those who administer public policy. The citizen is put to almost no bother or expense in getting his complaint before the Ombudsman. The scope of administrative activity which the Ombudsman will try to correct is very broad, ranging from violations of the law and the malicious abuse of authority to inefficiency, delay, and bad manners.

(2) If the Ombudsman believes that a complaint is obviously unfounded or that it is beyond his jurisdiction, he summarily dismisses it but not without explaining to the complainant the grounds for the dismissal. In the case of persons who have not exhausted other avenues of complaint, the Ombudsman, unless he decides to take up the case himself because of exceptional circumstances, explains to the complainant how to proceed through those avenues.

(3) When he believes that the complaint warrants it, the Ombudsman impartially, informally, inexpensively, and speedily investigates the matter. Investigation begins by asking an administrator for an explanation. If an explanation does not suffice, the Ombudsman has authority to look at the agency's files, to call witnesses and to request that the agency itself investigate the matter and report back to him. He thus relies for the most part on the agency under investigation to provide the factual basis for judging whether a complaint is justified.

(4) On his own initiative the Ombudsman may investigate administrative activities and practices which have come to his attention through some other source than a complaint.

(5) He may conduct inspections of administrative establishments within his jurisdiction. Although because of his relatively small staff and the lack of time, the Ombudsman is limited in the number and thoroughness of such inspections, still, they do provide a channel through which matters worthy of investigation can come to his attention.

(6) After conducting an enquiry, the Ombudsman has a variety of courses open to him. The one thing he cannot do—and this is an

extremely important characteristic of the institution—is to order an administrator to do anything. When the complaint is discovered to be unfounded, which is true in the overwhelming majority of cases because of the character of the environment in which the Ombudsman operates successfully, the Ombudsman explains to the complainant why the administrative act in question was valid. In some cases, even where he can find no legal or other imperfection in an administrative decision, the Ombudsman seeks to persuade the agency to make a different decision in order to save the complainant from needless hardship. Also in the case of groundless complaints, he sometimes nevertheless recommends to an agency ways for improving its operations. When the Ombudsman finds that a complaint is justified, he recommends to the agency a way to rectify its delinquency and often suggests steps to be taken to prevent a similar recurrence. The means recommended vary considerably according to the nature of the fault and may range from an administrator's apology to a complainant to the reversal of a decision or the payment of compensation. The Ombudsman has no authority to compel an administrative agency to accept his recommendations but relies on persuasion supported if need be by an appeal to legislative and public opinion. In Sweden and Finland where civil servants may be prosecuted for a much broader range of activities than in most countries and where the Ombudsmen have the authority to prosecute officials, the threat of prosecution has sometimes been used to oblige compliance with a recommendation. In every species of Ombudsman, criminal prosecution of an administrator can result from an Ombudsman's investigation. Even where the Ombudsman has no authority personally to prosecute, he may bring a crime committed by an administrator to the attention of the prosecuting authorities.

(7) The Ombudsman submits an annual report to the legislature and may report at other times at his discretion. These reports describe generally the Ombudsman's activity, record his criticisms, his recommendations, and administrative non-compliance with his recommendations, and may include proposals for legislative improvement of public administration.

DESIRABLE CONSEQUENCES

The task of describing the desirable consequences of the Ombudsman's activities is beset with normative and empirical problems. The normative problem of deciding which of the effects of the Ombudsman are indeed desirable can be avoided by assuming that the readers' values in this case are the same as the author's. This seems a perfectly warranted assumption since all of the consequences mentioned are related either directly or indirectly to the well-being of the members of a society. On the other hand, this is not to assume that all readers will assign the same degree of value to the various consequences. Such disagreement on ranking can possibly lead to a failure to agree on the advisability of introducing the Ombudsman into the United States.

In this essay, the empirical problem is of greater moment than the normative. Present knowledge of the consequences of Ombudsmen abroad is so limited that we might overlook desirable effects. Even where we are aware of them, it is sometimes very difficult to determine the degree to which an effect achieves the goal to which it is related. The latter difficulty is especially unfortunate, for in assessing the instrumental value of an institution, it makes a great difference whether it results in minimum or maximum attainment of the goals in respect of which it is assessed. The following list of desirable consequences of the Ombudsman was compiled from a survey of much of the writing on the institution. To further clarify the nature of the Ombudsman, the consequences are grouped under two broad social goals.

I. THE IMPROVEMENT OF PUBLIC ADMINISTRATION

(1) Public administrators do more than they would do in the absence of an Ombudsman to improve their agencies and especially their relations with their clients. Improvement stems partly from the Ombudsman's recommendations and partly from his mere existence, which prompts administrators to take more care. While there is considerable evidence that the Ombudsmen abroad do have this effect, there is also evidence that their success in this area is not so great as in that of affording protection to a citizen with a particular complaint. Professor Gellhorn has shown that civil servants are not always prepared to follow the Ombudsman's advice and change procedures and practices which in their eyes work satisfactorily; nor are they uniformly aware of the Ombudsman's presence. Many administrators are not even aware of reports by the Ombudsman relevant to their own activities. While it would be impossible to eliminate all the weakness in the Ombudsman's ability to improve administration, at least some of that displayed abroad could be reduced by larger and more effective circulation of the Ombudsman's findings and recommendations.

(2) The legislature is better prepared to oversee and improve administrative procedures and practices. This is the result of the Ombudsman's annual report which brings before the legislature administrative shortcomings which otherwise would not come to its attention. Through his handling of numerous complaints, the Ombudsman becomes aware of patterns of undesirable administrative behavior which isolated complaints would not reveal. While actual Ombudsmen have been able

to collect information useful for legislative activity, their own recommendations for legislation, according to Professor Gellhorn, have met with only limited success.

(3) People generally have greater faith and confidence in public administration which makes them more cooperative in their relations with civil servants and which improves the morale of the administrators themselves. The Ombudsman lessens public insecurity and irritation resulting from administrative activity and demonstrates to the public through his reports that the vast majority of the charges against civil servants are without foundation.

(4) Civil servants are shielded from unfounded accusations. While a complainant may not accept as valid an explanation from an agency itself, the same explanation coming from the obviously impartial Ombudsman is often accepted. Also the Ombudsman draws away from administrators and on to himself the complaints of persistent cranks.

II. THE PROTECTION AND PSYCHOLOGICAL SECURITY OF CITIZENS

(1) Individual grievances against unfair or abusive administrative activity are redressed. This protection is afforded through the complaint process described in paragraphs one, two, three, and six in the analysis of the structure of the Ombudsman. Just as the complaint process is the basic activity of the Ombudsman, this consequence of it can be viewed as fulfilling the basic goal of the institution. For the complaint procedure to achieve this goal most successfully, citizens with the types of complaints the Ombudsman should handle must be willing to bring them before him. This willingness depends upon citizens' awareness and understanding of, and respect for the institution. Equally important for success is the willingness of civil servants to accept the recommendations of the Ombudsman in particular cases. Impressionistic evidence from countries with Ombudsmen suggests that the institutions are widely known, respected, and seen as safeguards. As for the willingness of administrators abroad to accept recommendations concerning individual complaints, Professor Gellhorn has summed up the situation by writing, "The known instances of non-compliance with Ombudsmen's proposals have been few in number, picayune in content." [2]

(2) Citizens collectively are protected against improper and inefficient public administration. This protection is accomplished through reforms in administration which, as discussed above, can be attributed to the Ombudsman's activities.

(3) Citizens bringing complaints to the Ombudsman learn to have more effective relations with administrative agencies in the future. This occurs most obviously when an Ombudsman refuses to investigate

[2] Walter Gellhorn, *Ombudsmen and Others* (Cambridge, 1967), p. 437.

a complaint and explains to the complainant more appropriate channels, but it may be the effect of any of the Ombudsman's explanations to complainants.

(4) There is a lessening of fear and apprehension which people may have of a powerful, impersonal, and sometimes seemingly capricious bureaucracy which touches their lives at so many points. This is no mean achievement. "The political liberty of the subject," according to Montesquieu, "is a tranquillity of mind arising from the opinion each person has of his safety. In order to have this liberty, it is requisite the government be so constituted as one man need not be afraid of another." By being generally recognized in society as a fair and effective critic of administrative abuses and inefficiency, the Ombudsman increases that "tranquillity of mind" for which Montesquieu and other liberal writers have been so concerned.

UNDESIRABLE CONSEQUENCES

The very activities of an institution which are required in order to pursue its goals often have certain unintended, undesirable consequences which may frustrate the achievement of those or other goals. Although these dysfunctional consequences cannot be entirely eliminated, they can be minimized by the manner in which an institution is constructed and managed and by changes in the environment in which it operates. Most who have written about the Ombudsman have been concerned with emphasizing its virtues, and even those who oppose its introduction into their own countries tend to stress the difficulty in transferring it. The result has been that little has been said about any weaknesses inherent in the institution. A notable exception has been Professor Gellhorn, who, while advocating the introduction of the Ombudsman into the United States, has not neglected to indicate what he understands to be its undesirable consequences. The following list of such consequences is drawn from his works.

(1) The timidity of civil servants is increased, thus decreasing their effectiveness in executing public policies. By strengthening administration through criticizing improper behavior, the Ombudsman produces "hidden costs": "Awareness that someone is constantly looking over their shoulders causes some public officials to become too timid instead of too bold." [3]

(2) The Ombudsman's activities can lead to the creation of unnecessary red tape.

> Heavy reliance on the administrative files [in the conduct of the Ombudsman's investigations] has a side effect worth noting. In several countries officials assert that they have paid increasingly close attention to the desirability of preserving detailed records, so that were an external critic ever to

[3] Walter Gellhorn, *When Americans Complain* (Cambridge, 1966), p. 52.

ask questions about anything they have done, the files can provide complete answers. So far as this reinforces official care and accuracy, it is an obviously desirable development. If, as has apparently occurred in a few instances, adoration of the written word occupies so large a portion of the working day that accomplishments worth writing about become fewer and fewer, record keeping is a menace.[4]

(3) Occasionally Ombudsmen do more than they are suited to accomplish and attempt to influence decisions best left to administrators who are experts in handling certain matters.

> Overextension may unfortunately be an inherent element in the Ombudsman system. Those who vaunt the system greatly stress the importance of the Ombudsman's personality and his directly participating in every phase of official superintendence. This emphasis upon personalism may discourage the Ombudsman's using other governmental resources, lest he seem to have adopted "bureaucratic methods" and to be "passing the buck." . . . Ombudsmen everywhere tend to stretch themselves as close as possible to the unrealistic limits fixed by uninformed public desire. While unwillingness to stretch at all would be deplorable, willingness to stretch too far has its perils, too.[5]

(4) The Ombudsman's activities may decrease the support and admiration of administrators which he needs to operate successfully. This effect Professor Gellhorn characterizes as a "small danger" to look for when an Ombudsman is newly created, but it would seem there is a chance for it to occur at any period in the institution's life time when the Ombudsman becomes overzealous in finding defects in administration. "If the critic constantly depicts himself as a St. George slaying dragon after dragon, officials who do not relish being regarded as dragons may themselves become just a bit critical." [6]

(5) Since the Ombudsman is not himself engaged in administrative activity, administrators and legislatures are inclined to treat his general proposals for reform as impractical. Actual Ombudsmen have not had much opportunity for discussing their general proposals with administrators whose practical experience could be of use to them. If Professor Gellhorn is correct, the relative ineffectiveness of the Ombudsman in securing general administrative reforms is at least to some extent an inherent defect of the institution.[7]

(6) The citizens of a country with an Ombudsman may become complacent about governmental problems. "Too many persons seem willing to suppose, on much too little evidence, that God's in his

---

[4] *Ombudsmen and Others,* p. 432.
[5] *Ibid.,* p. 42.
[6] *Ibid.,* pp. 437-438.
[7] *When Americans Complain,* pp. 99-100.

heaven, all's right with the world of public administration so long as somebody like an Ombudsman is keeping an eye on operations." [8]

In an imperfect world one should not expect to find perfect institutions, but this is not to say that some institutions are not preferable to others. If in the countries having Ombudsmen the functional aspects of the institution did not far outweigh the dysfunctional, there would hardly be found the existing strong support for it among the citizens at large and even among civil servants. One must always weigh the desirable against the undesirable consequences of an institution, and available evidence indicates that Ombudsmen abroad contribute a great deal more to the attainment of important social goals than they do to their thwarting. It should also be kept in mind that the dysfunctional consequences of the Ombudsman's activity can be if not totally eliminated to some extent diminished.

ENVIRONMENTAL REQUISITES

Having determined the character of the Ombudsman and its desirable and undesirable consequences, we must now turn to the environmental conditions which must be present if the institution is to operate effectively to achieve its goals. It seems very likely that the success of the Ombudsman depends heavily upon its institutional and cultural environment, and some writers have laid equal emphasis on the geographic and demographic environment as well. The character of the requisite environment is implied in the above analysis and confirmed by the conditions in the five nations where the Ombudsman currently operates successfully.

The most obvious requisite is the existence of certain other governmental institutions: a bureaucracy to be complained about and improved and a law-making institution independent of and able to regulate the bureaucracy. Somewhat less obvious is the requirement that there be standards of fair and efficient administration accepted not only by the Ombudsman but generally by bureaucrats, legislators, and the rest of society. This consensus on norms is necessary partially because of the fact that the Ombudsman is not a large enough institution to handle the host of complaints arising from a corrupt bureaucracy and partially because of the fact that it can affect the actions of administrators and legislators only through persuasion. This dependence of the Ombudsman's persuasive powers on his sharing values and norms with the large majority of the bureaucrats with whom he deals has led Professor Gellhorn to conclude perceptively that the Ombudsman will succeed best where he is least needed. The unfortunate correlative of this conclusion is that in the African, Asian, and Latin American world where the goals of the Ombudsman

[8] *Ibid.,* p. 53.

are so very far from being fulfilled, the institution would seem to have the least chance of success. Even in Scandinavia and New Zealand discrepancies between administrative norms and those of the Ombudsman have diminished the latter's effectiveness in some areas such as the reduction of bureaucratic secrecy and police excesses.

Besides an efficient and honest bureaucracy, the successful Ombudsman also requires the presence in his environment of other institutions which contribute to the protection and psychological security of the members of the society and to the improvement of its public administration. No one has ever claimed that the Ombudsman can go very far toward achieving these goals by himself. Because of the size of the institution and its limited powers it can only supplement the contributions of proper rules of administrative procedure, a well recruited and trained civil service, and other institutions of complaint handling and administrative reform.

Although we have considered at length the character of the Ombudsman including its consequences and goals, nothing has yet been said of how the office is filled. Unless the Ombudsman is allowed to choose his own successor, which no one has ever contemplated, the choice must be made by other institutions in the environment. But which? If we look to the experience of the five well established Ombudsman systems, the answer appears simple enough. All are chosen by popularly elected legislative assemblies or (in the case of Sweden) by the committee of such an assembly. Many commentators believe this mode of selection to be essential, because they see the Ombudsman as an agent of the legislature. He is indeed described as such in the legal provisions governing the existing offices. Thus the Swedish constitution describes the Ombudsman as the "attorney of Parliament" who is to act under instructions issued by it, while in New Zealand and the United Kingdom his official English title is "Parliamentary Commissioner." Must we then conclude that any Ombudsman who is not selected by the legislature is a faulty specimen? Our analysis of the structure and consequences of the Ombudsman suggests that we need not.

All that the Ombudsman requires from the standpoint of his selection, maintenance, and removal are methods which will not lessen his ability to make a maximum contribution toward the achievement of the institution's goals. It is especially important that the Ombudsman both be and appear to be impartial. Thus to choose him through a popular election would not seem appropriate, as it would run the strong risk of involving him in partisan politics. Also it would seem inappropriate for the Ombudsman to be chosen by the bureaucracy itself, the parts of which he is to supervise. Even in these cases, one should be cautious in stating categorically that an Ombudsman so chosen could not perform successfully. A great deal depends on environmental conditions, as is shown by the effective operations and popular prestige of the French *Conseil d'Etat.* This institution functions in part similarly to the Ombudsman but it is composed mostly of high civil servants, who reach their positions through competitive examinations and who may be dismissed at any time by a decree of the Council of Ministers. For years Anglo-American opinion was intensely suspicious of this body, which appeared to fall so short of the requirements for impartiality, but today students of the subject have almost nothing but praise for the *Conseil d'Etat,* the impartiality of which they no longer doubt. In fact its members are not dismissed by the Council of Ministers for the way they decide cases, and the institution is seen by scholars and the French people as independent and scrupulously fair in its handling of citizens' complaints against administration.

The *Conseil d'Etat* does not, as it first appeared to do, violate the ancient principle of "natural justice" that a man should not be a judge in his own case. This is because the members of the council, although civil servants, do not identify their interest with the civil servant whose behavior is the subject of complaint. When this identity of interest does occur the principle is violated, and this fact is the basis for the need for complaint procedures outside of the agencies complained about. Thus, in 1964 Sir Guy Powles spoke before the Canadian Bar Association of his experiences as the New Zealand Ombudsman:

> In dealing with the large number of complaints against discretionary administrative action, it has become clear that careful and often repeated review of a decision within a Department is no guarantee of the wisdom and fairness of the ultimate decision. The first decision, even if made by delegation or in the ordinary course of administration at a relatively low level, tends to generate its own defences within a Department—a process of rationalization can generally bring out arguments in favour of the original decision that may not have been known to the person who made it.

The tendency toward partiality within the agency probably can be offset to a considerable degree when the internal judge is clearly detached from the other officials who carry out the regular activities of the agency. Indeed such an executive official, given authority to accept and investigate complaints concerning several administrative agencies, to initiate investigations of them, and to report his findings and recommendations publicly can in fact be an Ombudsman as described in this essay. Because of historical developments, both Sweden and Finland have such Ombudsmen in their executively appointed Chancellors of Justice, who, while having certain duties and powers not possessed by the legislatively appointed Ombudsmen, also function as Ombudsmen.

If he is to be an impartial judge of complaints against administration, the Ombudsman's decisions should not depend on any institution, governmental or private. It is for this reason that in the five countries where the Ombudsman is appointed by the legislature and subject to its general instructions, neither the legislature nor any of its members ever intervene to influence particular decisions. It seems very probable that if they ever should intervene public opinion would be outraged. Besides the legislature, the Ombudsman must be independent of political parties and interest groups. These two institutional requisites of any large modern political system have both shown themselves capable of reducing and sometimes destroying the independence of other institutions. In Scandinavia and New Zealand this has not been the case with the Ombudsmen. It would seem that two circumstances protect the Ombudsman from penetration by parties and interest groups. The institution is protected by the generally accepted norms which require its independence from outside intervention. For parties or groups to attempt to control the decisions of the Ombudsman is to invite the loss of the popular support they need for achieving their objectives. This risk is hardly worth taking in view of the nature of the Ombudsman's activities, which involve making recommendations in cases usually of little individual importance.

One of the most debated aspects of transferring the Ombudsman has been whether its portability is considerably limited by geographic and demographic conditions. All five countries with successfully operating Ombudsmen are of relatively small territorial dimensions and contain populations of under eight million persons. Also in each of these countries the Ombudsman personally reads every incoming complaint before assigning it to his staff for investigation and he personally takes a hand in all important cases. These facts seem to be the basis for two current opinions upon which is founded the conclusion that the Ombudsman can function successfully only in very small nations. First it is asserted that the institution can gain necessary respect and acceptance only if it is presided over by a single man performing in much the same manner as the existing Ombudsmen. Naturally this is impossible in larger nations. Secondly, it is alleged that in a large nation the personnel required to carry out the functions of an Ombudsman would become so large as to constitute a bureaucracy itself.

These assertions and the conclusion derived from them have been strongly contested. Professor Donald Rowat has characterized as "a lot of sentimental twaddle" the emphasis placed by some writers on the Ombudsman's personal touch, which he believes to be far less important than the impartiality of the office. Rather than praise the single Ombudsman's personal handling of important cases, Rowat believes that it would be advantageous in populous countries to have a commission of three Ombudsmen, who would handle less important cases individually and more important cases collectively.[9] Professor Gellhorn has observed that historically collegial bodies have won for themselves just as much respect as single officers and that a collegial Ombudsman would not be an administrative bureau since the functions of the two types of institutions are quite different. Sweden, we should remind ourselves, already has a number of Ombudsmen: a civil Ombudsman, his deputy, a military Ombudsman, and the Chancellor of Justice. The fear that in a large nation the Ombudsman, singular or plural, would preside over an enormous staff appears to stem from a misunderstanding of the institution, which is viewed as closely supervising the entire bureaucracy through its own investigatory apparatus. The Ombudsman, however, does not function and is not equipped to function as such an inspectorate of administration, despite what some legal descriptions may suggest to the contrary. Even in the investigations it does carry out, it relies primarily on the files, reports, and letters of others. Certainly one can expect the number of Ombudsmen and their staffs to grow with an increase in the population they serve, but whatever the institution's size, it will always be far smaller than the administration it oversees.

When all is said and done, the question whether the dimensions of population and size of a country after a certain point can limit the transferability of the Ombudsman remains unanswered. What can be said with considerable certainty is that the institution can operate successfully with areas and populations much larger than those with which it currently operates.

Do We Need Ombudsmen?

That the United States needs some means for reforming and redressing complaints about public administration is so evident that there is no necessity to discuss it at length. No modern industrial nation can dispense with the many services and regulations rendered by efficient and impersonal large-scale public organizations, yet it seems abundantly clear that the men who manage these organizations do not always act so as to fulfill social goals.

[9] Donald C. Rowat, "The Parliamentary Ombudsmen: Should the Scandinavian Scheme be Transplanted?" *International Review of Administrative Sciences, XVIII* (1962), 404-405.

Sometimes this pathological behavior results from administrators failing to live up to the type of behavior appropriate to bureaucratic organizations. For example, if a man in administrative office does not adopt the bureaucratic role, which requires obedience to legal rules and the impersonal treatment of the public, one can expect to find favoritism for the office holder's family, friends, and groups with whom he identifies himself and discrimination against those individuals and groups he dislikes. Although this pathology of "under-organization" would appear to decline in more modern societies, no nation including the United States has come near to eliminating it entirely. Indeed, in some areas of this country it provides the basis for a method of complaint about administrative activity, as when a man calls a friend at City Hall to redress a grievance caused by another official.

The other major form of bureaucratic pathology has been called "over-organization." [10] When exaggerated, behavior expected and typical of bureaucratic organizations creates dysfunctional effects with respect to the achievement of an institution's goals. Thus, conformity to legal rules and equal treatment of the public is highly desirable up to a point, but if carried to extremes such behavior can cause needless delay and bother to the public and an unwillingness of bureaucrats to make decisions which minimize individual hardship. Or, to take another example, while an administrative organization cannot publicize all of its activities, bureaucratic secrecy often arises from laziness and overprotectiveness and extends further than need be, causing the public bewilderment and dissatisfaction. Both types of pathological behavior may be limited by changes in large-scale organizations and their environments, but, because of the imperfections inherent in all human organizations there will always be some need for methods of correcting them. In the United States this need is suggested by the variety of institutions currently striving to meet it, which brings us to the question, *Is there a need in this country, at the national, state, or local levels of government, for a well-functioning Ombudsman in addition to or as a partial modification of existing institutions redressing complaints against administration and improving administrative practices and procedures?*

Two approaches might be taken to answer this question. By carefully surveying public opinion, one might answer such questions as whether people feel as threatened and alienated from our bureaucratic institutions as some writers would have us think, how satisfied people are with existing means for handling their complaints against administration, and whether they feel the need for more protection. Research of this kind is concerned mainly with the psychological need

---

[10] Robert K. Merton, etc. (eds.), *Reader in Bureaucracy* (Glencoe, 1952), p. 396.

of the citizens of the United States, which even if accurately determined does not provide us with all the information we require to adequately assess the performance of existing American institutions relevant to our enquiry. Public opinion cannot tell us whether or not the introduction of the Ombudsman into the United States will significantly improve the reform of and handling of complaints against public administration, for there is no reason to believe that the mass of the American people have the knowledge to make such a judgment. To answer such a question requires research into the character and consequences of existing American institutions.

PUBLIC OPINION

Almost no attempt has been made to survey opinion in this country about the need for an Ombudsman. In late 1965, the Gallup Poll asked two questions to see whether or not Americans were in favor of the idea of an Ombudsman to handle complaints against federal public officials. (1) "A proposal has been made to set up an independent agency in Washington to handle the complaints of citizens who think they have not been treated properly by government officials. Do you think this is a good idea or a poor idea?" (2) "As you may know, Congressmen spend about half their time doing errands and favors for people in their districts. To give Congressmen more time to consider new legislation it has been suggested that all letters and requests—except those dealing with policy matters—be turned over to a central bureau for handling." To the first question, which was intended to elicit opinion about an Ombudsman as described in this essay, 42 per cent of the respondents thought the proposal was a good idea, 29 per cent a poor idea, and 29 percent had no opinion. To the second question, which referred to a modification of the Ombudsman suggested by Congressman Henry Reuss, the response was 46 per cent in favor, 41 per cent opposed, and 13 per cent with no opinion.[11]

This poll is more useful for illustrating pitfalls in surveying public opinion than providing us with the information we need. The two questions are phrased so differently—the second unlike the first containing an argument as well as the loaded term "central bureau"—that it is not surprising the two patterns of answers are different. The poll is a healthy reminder that the way in which questions are put has a great deal to do with the answers they receive. Still, one aspect of the answers is worthy of attention. In the case of both questions between 40 and 50 per cent of the respondents in declaring for the proposals may be revealing that they believe they are not adequately protected

[11] Quoted in R. H. Davidson, D. M. Kovenock, and M. K. O'Leary, *Congress in Crisis: Politics and Congressional Reform* (Belmont, 1966), p. 65.

by existing complaint procedures. This is especially likely with respect
to the 42 per cent who gave an affirmative reply to the first question.

Another body of survey data, not collected with the Ombudsman
in mind, casts further light on opinion in this country relevant to
determining psychological need for an Ombudsman. In their outstanding work on the political culture of five nations,[12] Professors
Gabriel A. Almond and Sydney Verba, fortunately for our purposes,
asked among many others the following questions: "Suppose there
were some questions that you had to take to a government office—for
example, a tax question or a housing regulation. Do you think you
would be given equal treatment—I mean, would you be treated as well
as anyone else?" "If you had trouble with the police—a traffic violation
maybe, or were accused of a minor offense—do you think you would
be given equal treatment? That is, would you be treated as well as
anyone else?" The questions were asked to a sample of Americans in
1960 and their answers appear below.

TABLE I: EXPECTATION OF TREATMENT BY GOVERNMENTAL BUREAUCRACY AND POLICE

Per cent who say	Bureaucracy	Police
They expect equal treatment	83	85
They don't expect equal treatment	9	8
Depends	4	5
Don't know	4	2
Total Per Cent	100	100

Clearly a large majority of Americans are not afraid of favoritism or
discrimination in their encounters with bureaucracy and the police,
but that still leaves about 20 million of the 200 million people in this
country who do not expect equal treatment. The above questions were
followed by two others. "If you explained your point of view to the
officials, what effect do you think it would have? Would they give
your point of view serious consideration, would they pay only a little
attention, or would they ignore what you had to say?" "If you explained your point of view to the police, what effect do you think it
would have? Would they . . . [same choice as before]?" Table II shows
the American answers.

[12] G. A. Almond and S. Verba, *The Civic Culture* (Princeton, 1963), Ch. 4. The
two tables in this paragraph are slight adaptations of tables 2 and 3 of that chapter.

TABLE II: *AMOUNT OF CONSIDERATION EXPECTED FOR POINT OF VIEW FROM BUREAUCRACY AND POLICE*

Per cent who expect	Bureaucracy	Police
Serious consideration for point of view	48	56
A little attention	31	22
To be ignored	6	11
Depends	11	9
Don't know	4	2
Total Per Cent	100	100

It appears that about one-third of the people of the United States expect little or no attention to be given to their point of view by the bureaucracy and police, while only about a half expect serious attention.

The two tables as well as other data in the Almond and Verba study suggest that extreme and sweeping statements about fear of bureaucratic authority in the United States are very misleading. A sizable majority of Americans believe that both their national and local governments tend on the whole to improve conditions. On the other hand, the data do indicate that a small percentage but numerically large number of Americans expect to be treated unfairly by administrators while far more see bureaucracy as not taking them sufficiently into consideration while making its decisions. These are probably the kinds of people who in the Gallup Poll showed an interest in the Ombudsman idea. Whether or not the institution would actually allay their apprehension about administrative agencies cannot, of course, be demonstrated until the Ombudsman is tried.

EXISTING MEANS FOR REDRESSING GRIEVANCES
AND IMPROVING ADMINISTRATION

Surveying public opinion will not take us very far in ascertaining the need for an Ombudsman in the United States. Such an approach must be accompanied by careful enquiry into the effectiveness of the current means in this country for improving public administration and redressing complaints against it. As argued in Chapter 3, much research remains to be done before an adequate appraisal of this effectiveness can be made. All that can be undertaken in this essay is a brief consideration of the general nature of these means in order to determine if it is likely that they exclude the need for additional methods.

Administrative Agencies—Channels for citizens' complaints are found within agencies at all levels of government. As indispensable as such channels are, they suffer from the inherent defect of bias in favor of the agency or at least of being suspected of bias. Only a separate inspectorate in a very large organization seems capable of largely overcoming this defect. What seems to be needed in the United States is an institution such as the Ombudsman which can be appealed to by a citizen who believes he has not been fairly treated by an internal grievance handler. The improvement of the internal channels, although not eliminating the need for an external channel, could very much reduce its work load. As for administrative reform, in the American as well as in every other reasonably healthy bureaucracy important proposals for improvement come from within the agencies, but it is also evident even the most alert agency can become blind to defects more apparent to outsiders.[13]

The Courts—No one would deny that the courts of the United States are important avenues of complaint against administration and that through their decisions they improve administrative procedures. When a civil servant is believed to have acted without legal authority, to have failed to have carried out a duty defined precisely by law, or to have needlessly harmed someone's person or property, Americans turn to the courts for redress.

There are, however, two characteristics of judicial redress in this country which prevent many people with complaints against administration from going to court. First, there is the money and time involved. The likelihood of a person taking a case before a court seems to be directly related to his income, a pattern which has been only partly changed by legal aid schemes, which do not serve all areas of the country, are restricted in the assistance they grant, and have such low limits for eligibility as to assist only the very poor. Compared to cases taken before Ombudsmen, most complaints taken to court involve the complainant in a much greater expenditure of time as well as money—time spent in consulting with lawyers and testifying in court. Secondly, even when a legitimate complaint against administrative activity is brought before them, American courts are often not in a position to provide redress. As a summary of the problem puts it, "The power of the courts to review administrative conduct is limited . . . by statutory and judicial restrictions based on considerations of finality, exhaustion of administrative remedies, standing, and def-

---

[13] See Kenneth Culp Davis, "Ombudsmen in America: Officers to Criticize Administrative Action," *University of Pennsylvania Law Review*, 109 (June, 1961), 1057-1076, for organizations which have been created, or proposed to be created, as separate institutions within the executive branch of government to study and improve administrative procedures.

erence to administrative discretion. . . . Nor can the courts deal with issues of efficiency, rudeness, or unnecessary red tape, issues which may be paramount in the eyes of the citizen." [14] In the improvement of administration the courts are hampered by being obliged to wait until the right case comes before them before they can lay down certain procedural requirements or invalidate illegal practices. Also the courts' methods for reforming administration sometimes have rather strange side effects, as when "they have set lawbreakers free in order to drive home a lesson to policemen who had grown careless of citizens' rights." [15]

Grand Juries—The defects in the courts' performance of the reform function are not to be found in their investigatory arm, the grand jury, a body of citizens empaneled both to bring formal charges against suspects in criminal cases and to uncover criminal activity within the courts' jurisdictions. Equipped with a court's power to subpoena witnesses and papers, the grand jury is supposed to discover criminal activity and then bring charges against those engaged in it. In the case of public officers, even when there is no evidence upon which to base a criminal charge, the grand jury may nevertheless issue reports publicly criticizing persons and institutions. At their best, grand juries have been able to perform valuable service in revealing and suggesting means for reforming administrative abuses and inefficiencies. For example, in June 1967, the New York County grand jury issued a presentment which, besides indicting fourteen inspectors from the Buildings Department for having taken bribes from landlords, criticized in detail the conditions in the department which had led to corruption. Here would seem to be a report of which any Ombudsman would be proud, yet it would be far from accurate to describe the grand jury as the equivalent of an Ombudsman.

The grand jury is not as free from partisan motivation as it might first appear. Far more often than not it performs not as an independent agency but as an appendage of the district attorney's office, upon which it depends for the cases brought before it and their investigation. "The district attorney," a favorable commentator on the grand jury has written, "because of his access to information, prestige as an important governmental official, and familiarity with grand jury procedure, tends to direct the grand jury's operations." [16] District attorneys in America are often deeply involved in party politics. The grand jury's dependence on the public prosecutor is partially the result

---

[14] Richard I. Aaron, "Utah Ombudsman: The American Proposals," *Utah Law Review* (March, 1967), 38-39.

[15] Gellhorn, *When Americans Complain*, p. 32.

[16] "The Grand Jury as an Investigatory Body," *Harvard Law Review*, 74 (January, 1961), 596.

of another way in which the institution differs from the Ombudsman.
The jurors are inexperienced amateurs picked to serve usually for
only a few months in a role for which they have no special skills; the
Ombudsman is a specialist experienced in overseeing bureaucratic
activity and able to call upon a well trained staff for assistance. In
respect to the redressing of individual complaints the two institutions
are even more unalike. While the Ombudsman is mainly concerned
with swiftly and effectively processing a sizable number of complaints,
the grand jury is formed to carry out a few rather lengthy investigations. Indeed, there has been some legal question as to whether it
should even receive communications from private persons.[17]

Government Law Officers—Every state has an attorney general and
district attorney who among other activities may receive complaints
about alleged criminal conduct by public officials. When he enquired
among attorneys general of the various states about where citizens
were most likely to go with complaints against state administration
agencies, Professor Richard I. Aaron was told that one frequent place
was their own offices.[18] Judging from the experience of California, one
gets the impression that the attorneys general are frequently able to
do nothing for the complainants. According to State Senator Mervyn
M. Dymally, most of the many complaints received by the California
Attorney General's office are answered, "I regret to have to inform you
that it is neither the duty nor the privilege of this office, as attorneys
for the state, to answer enquiries of this nature from private persons." [19] Whether the attorneys general of other states are able to do
more for complainants is not known, but the nature of their jurisdiction alone would make it unlikely. District attorneys are principally
concerned with prosecuting violations of their states' criminal laws,
but, as we have seen, they also play an important part in the investigatory function of grand juries. Unfortunately, the impartiality
of all state law officers is too often undermined by motives of political
or legal career advancement. The investigation of another government
agency may stem more from a desire to attack a political opponent or
to inflate one's reputation than to improve the quality of administration.

Chief Executives—This category includes the President of the United
States, governors of states, and local chief executives. All are in a
position to initiate investigations of administrative practices and to
varying extents all do, sometimes with salutary effects; but administrative reform must compete with the many other problems with

[17] W. J. Fremon, "Private Communications with Grand Juries," *Journal of Criminal Law and Criminology, 38* (May-June, 1947), 43-48.

[18] Aaron, "Utah Ombudsman," 36-37.

[19] Testifying before the California Assembly Committee on Government Organization. Los Angeles, September 26, 1966.

which chief executives are concerned. As heads of administration, all chief executives receive in the mail which floods into their offices complaints about administrative activity. Letters of complaint to the White House or the governor's mansion routinely are taken care of by administrative assistants, who simply send them on to the agencies concerned to prepare answers. In effect, without knowing it the complainant usually is addressing his complaint to the very people he believes to have injured him. This also seems true of most localities, although some have created specialized agencies for dealing more expertly with complaints. Thus, Mayor John V. Lindsay of New York City set up "little city halls" in three sections of the city, which function somewhat like Ombudsmen in the manner in which they handle complaints. Both as to handling complaints and improving administration, chief executives at the state and local levels suffer from a weakness from which the President is relatively free, for they have far from complete control over administrative activity at their levels. It is still the case in a large majority of states that the attorney general, the state treasurer, and the secretary of state are popularly elected, and in about half the superintendent of education is elected. This is not to mention the numerous administrative boards and commissions which do not come under the governor's authority. In many localities the situation is even more extreme than at the state level, for the weak mayor-council form of city government and the typical form of county government are even less integrated.

Legislatures—Taken all together, the American legislative assembly, its committees, and its individual members are very important in reforming public administration and handling complaints about bureaucratic activity. As a law-making body, the legislature within limits set by the relevant constitution can create and eliminate administrative agencies and prescribe rules by which they should operate. At the state and local levels the limits can be considerable. Through the activities of its committees, the legislature can oversee the actual conduct of administration, and through the "case work" of its members it can handle a large number of individual complaints. A noted student of the United States Congress has observed,

> Today "legislative oversight" has become *a* if not *the* principal activity of the standing committees of both houses. . . . With a mandate to watch continuously, equipped with staffs and funds, "committee government" in our time has thus acquired new significance as a system of inspection and review of administrative performance. The Eighty-third Congress alone authorized upwards of 7,500,000 dollars for various probes.[20]

[20] George B. Galloway, *History of the House of Representatives* (New York, 1961), pp. 185, 188. See also Samuel F. Huntington, "Congressional Responses to the Twentieth Century," in David B. Truman (ed.), *The Congress and America's Future* (Prentice-Hall, Inc., 1965), pp. 5-31.

Clearly the investigations carried on by Congress differ considerably
from those of an Ombudsman, whose investigations, should the office
be created nationally, would complement rather than compete with
those of Congress. With all the power and techniques at their disposal,
Congressional committees may still overlook the kinds of administrative
deficiencies encountered by an Ombudsman during the performance
of his duties. State legislative committees also oversee administration
but not so effectively as Congress because of the shortcomings in so
many of the state legislatures which reformers have assailed for years:
biennial sessions, short sessions, and the rapid turnover in and poor
quality of membership.

Legislators—To an apparently increasing degree the 535 members
of the Congress of the United States and the approximately 7700 state
legislators individually perform among a number of other functions
that of handling citizens' grievances against public administration. In
several respects the legislator's performance of this function resembles
that of the Ombudsman: both provide quick service for the complainant at no trouble or expense to himself and both rely heavily for
information upon the administrative agencies themselves. On the
other hand, what is known of the "case work" of congressmen suggests
that there are a number of defects which do not appear in the
Ombudsman's operations.

(1) A serious defect is the lack of uniformity even among members
of the same legislative body in the manner in which complaints are
handled. Partisan discrimination does not appear to be a serious
problem, but it is probable that legislators, obsessed as most of them
are with re-election, are reluctant to handle complaints which may
lose them votes. More importantly, the kind of consideration given
to a complaint and its chance of success vary according to the size and
quality of a legislator's staff, the kinds of contacts they have with administrative agencies, and the degree to which the legislator himself
takes a hand in enquiring about a complaint.

(2) Because of their awareness of the legislator's power and his
desire to please his constituents, bureaucrats may actually reverse valid
decisions. Charles L. Clapp describes this danger as arising even when
a legislator simply expresses routine interest in a case. "Unclear regarding the true interest of the congressman but reluctant to chance
antagonizing him, the agency may bend regulations as much as possible
in determining disposition of the case." [21] While this kind of influence
may seem fine from the standpoint of a particular complainant, it

---

[21] Charles L. Clapp, *The Congressman: His Work As He Sees It* (Washington,
1963), p. 81. See also Gellhorn, *When Americans Complain*, pp. 57-94, 125-130; and
Kenneth G. Olson, "The Service Function of the United States Congress," in Alfred
de Grazia (ed.), *Congress: The First Branch of Government* (1966), pp. 337-374.

can lessen the ability of administrative agencies to achieve their legitimate goals.

(3) At the same time as the legislator is in a better position than the Ombudsman to prejudice administrative decisions, he is in a worse position to judge effectively the validity of a complaint. The legislator and his staff are generally not so well qualified to make such judgments and they do not have such access to agency files.

(4) There are certain inevitable or highly likely inefficiencies which result from legislators handling complaints. It takes them and to a greater extent their staffs away from performing other important functions such as law-making and generally overseeing the administration. The extreme decentralization inherent in the system leads to the employment of larger personnel for grievance handling than would be required in a centralized system. In the case of a bicameral legislature, the same complaint may actually be processed by two legislators. Since the principle motive behind the legislator's case work is to build and maintain political support by doing favors, legislators are inclined to send all complaints presented to them on to the administrators who are needlessly bothered with trivial or obviously baseless complaints.

(5) Defenders of legislators' case work often argue that it has the important side effect of assisting the legislature in its tasks of administrative oversight and reform. While to some extent it must be true that the information acquired by legislators in handling complaints can be of use in the performance of other functions, it is doubtful if this contribution is usually very significant. Too often legislators are interested simply in doing favors for constituents and do not follow up the implications of complaints to gain a better understanding of administrative problems. Legislators usually leave most complaints for their staffs to take care of and consequently they themselves have only superficial knowledge of the administrative activity involved. The information legislators do attain is not applied to the improvement of administration as effectively as would the same information in the possession of a single specialized organization, which would be able to spot patterns of poor administration invisible to the legislator, who can see only a tiny part of the whole.

Much that has been said of the congressman's activity as grievance man can also be said about the state legislator. Because of the more rapid turnover in office, less adequate staff, and the generally poorer quality of the legislators themselves, the state legislator is in a worse position than his national counterpart to settle complaints against administration.

Private Activity—Thus far we have been considering public institutions in America which handle individual complaints against public administration or take a part in improving bureaucracy generally.

There are, in addition, private organizations which assist in the performance of these functions. Research institutes study possible reforms. Interest groups of various sorts will sometimes intercede for a member or client who believes himself wronged by the governmental bureaucracy. The American Civil Liberties Union and the National Association for the Advancement of Colored People are well known examples. Another kind of institution which has long played a part in improving governmental administration as well as voicing and investigating the complaints of individuals has been the American press, especially when the crusade has been likely to increase circulation.

A recent development in the newspaper handling of complaints has been a daily column specializing in complaints and problems of readers. Often going under the name of "Action Line," the columns encourage readers to call or write them about problems, which often are sent in by the hundreds each day, as discussed in Chapter 4. Reporters are employed to investigate complaints and to recommend to their source methods for redress. From what is known of them, "Action Lines" do appear to have been frequently successful in getting local administrators to correct minor mistakes, but it is misleading to refer to them as private Ombudsmen as is sometimes done. They have neither the Ombudsman's expertise nor his means for investigation. Rather than restrict themselves solely to complaints against public administration, they also accept those against private organizations as well as simply supply information on all manner of subjects including surgery for protruding ears and where to get tickets for a garden show. While the contribution of the "Action Line" should not be disparaged simply because it often concerns itself with trivia and is very much involved in promoting circulation, one can say with confidence that it is not a substitute for an Ombudsman.

From this brief survey of the institutions in the United States currently assisting in the achievement of the two social goals of the redress of grievances against public administration and its general reform, a case can surely be made that there is room for improvement. Some improvement can come through further perfecting existing institutions; yet the survey suggests that these institutions have inherent limitations and defects which can never be fully overcome.

If we conclude that another kind of institution is required, we are not necessarily committed to the Ombudsman, for it is possible that some other institution would better fulfill our needs. Here people concerned about these needs must be careful not to fall into a permanent state of indecision. No amount of research into the Ombudsman and other foreign institutions can bring complete certainty as to whether the institution we adopt is best suited to our needs. Some persons oppose the introduction of the Ombudsman on the grounds that it is a palliative which would prevent the adoption of the institution which is really needed. That institution is usually said to be an administrative court of the French sort. If it is true that a possible dysfunctional effect of the Ombudsman is to blind people to the need of administrative reform, then there is something to this objection if it can also be shown that the Ombudsman's contribution is trivial, that an administrative court's contribution is very large and supersedes that of the Ombudsman, and that there is a strong likelihood that the adoption of the Ombudsman would prevent that of an administrative court. However, if the proponents of the Ombudsman are correct—and further research properly financed could fairly soon provide a reasonably firm basis for confirming or refuting their position—the institution can make significant contributions to our needs. Compared to the Ombudsman, the *Conseil d'Etat* and the lower administrative courts of France, as admirable as they seem to be, are not always as inexpensive, quick, and simple for the complainant, nor can they redress such a wide scope of complaints or initiate action themselves. That the administrative court does not render an Ombudsman superfluous is also strongly suggested by the fact that in Sweden and Finland both institutions function and are seen to do so successfully. As for the palliative effect of the Ombudsman, the same can be said of the administrative courts. According to a close student of the French system, it places so much stress on judicial techniques that it neglects the improvement of administrative procedural safeguards.[22] The effect of either the Ombudsman or the administrative court in inhibiting further reform is an unfortunate but hardly insurmountable barrier. If the need is great and persistent enough, it is very likely to be met. Actually the greatest barrier to the introduction of an administrative court system into the United States seems not to be the Ombudsman but the fact that it would require a rather extensive restructuring of our judicial system involving a sizable limitation on the jurisdiction of our regular judges. Such a prerequisite would very probably encounter powerful opposition.

Can the Ombudsman Be Transferred?

Assuming the need for a successful Ombudsman in the United States, the question still remains as to whether or not it can be transferred here. The rest of this essay is concerned with problems which might prevent or cause difficulty in the transfer.

The phrase "to transfer an institution," if it is to be of use, must

[22] Prosper Weil, "The Strength and Weakness of French Administrative Law," *Cambridge Law Journal* (November, 1965), 256-257.

refer to a good deal more than the decision to transfer. In the case of the Ombudsman, a successful transfer can be said to take place only after it has functioned according to the model presented at the beginning of this chapter for such a period of time that it is reasonable to conclude it will continue to do so indefinitely. Only after his office had been in operation for five years did the New Zealand Ombudsman state in his 1967 Report (p. 5):

> With the continued cordial cooperation of Ministers and the sincere and willing assistance of the Departments and organizations subject to jurisdiction, the Office continues to run according to a fairly stable pattern. The proportion of justified complaints to those investigated remains steady, and this proportion bears a remarkable similarity to those obtained in Ombudsmen's offices overseas. The institution seems to have taken root.

Of course, successful transference does not preclude subsequent development into a rather different kind of organization. An institution can be transformed into a different institution without being transferred, as is shown by the Swedish Justitieombudsman which has undergone very significant structural changes since its origin in 1809. Indeed the nineteenth century JO scarcely qualifies as an Ombudsman as described in this essay.

As we saw earlier, for the Ombudsman to function successfully depends upon its environment. The United States and the existing Ombudsman countries are similar enough in their social, economic, and political institutions, perceptions, and values to encourage a fair amount of optimism about the successful introduction of the Ombudsman into this country. If this similarity did not exist, one would expect any attempt to create an American Ombudsman to result in not a transfer but a transformation of the institution, as so often happens when a decision is made to set up the institutions of the modern industrial world in far less developed areas. Still, some aspects of the American environment are different, or alleged to be different, from that of Scandinavia and New Zealand and these deserve closer scrutiny.

THE PROBLEM OF THE SIZE OF THE UNITED STATES

One of the most often mentioned reasons for doubting that the Ombudsman can be transferred to the United States has been the great size of the territory and population of the country as a whole and of some of its states. It was argued above that to a considerable extent this doubt is based upon a misunderstanding of the institution which holds that there can only be one Ombudsman and that he must take an important part in handling every complaint. Actually, only about a fifth of the states are larger in population than Sweden. In very large states such as California and New York—each with a population of about twenty million—there would be a need for three or four Ombudsmen, each possibly specializing in certain kinds of complaints or taking care of territorial subdivisions but coming together to consider the hard cases. The United States as a whole with its population of 200 million may well cause the most fervent advocate of the Ombudsman to have doubts about its applicability at the national level of government. Ombudsmen abroad have not received many more than 1000 complaints a year. Professor Gellhorn has estimated from his sampling of complaints to United States congressmen "that well over 200,000 complaints about administration reach congressional offices in the course of a year." [23] If we accept this estimate and assume that after the adoption of a national Ombudsman with jurisdiction over the entire federal administration even a small majority of such complaints would be taken care of by the Ombudsman's office, the magnitude of the problem becomes only too clear. Could a federal Ombudsman cover administration without becoming a slow cumbersome organization composed perhaps of two or three tiers of Ombudsmen? We should not be too hasty in answering this question in the negative, for modern forms of transportation, communications, and information storage and retrieval may allow the Ombudsman to have a far larger case load than one would assume from foreign experience. Still, given the great uncertainty surrounding this matter, it would probably be prudent in introducing an Ombudsman at the federal level to follow the course suggested by Senator Edward V. Long's bill, S.1195 (1967), which applies to a limited list of governmental agencies. If the institution later showed a capability for handling a greater complaint load without appreciable loss of efficiency, other agencies could be added to its jurisdiction.

THE PROBLEM OF THE OMBUDSMAN'S COMPATIBILITY WITH AMERICAN POLITICAL PRINCIPLES AND INSTITUTIONS

The decision to introduce the Ombudsman depends upon the institution's not disrupting the desirable aspects of our present political system. Few Americans would accept an institution seen as violating the principles of federalism and the separation of powers or which considerably changed the form of government said to be based upon them.

It is difficult to see how the Ombudsman could affect adversely American federalism, for the jurisdiction of the federal and state Ombudsmen would be limited respectively to the federal and state bureaucracies. Indeed, federalism facilitates the introduction of the Ombudsman into a large country by breaking the country and public administration into separate independent parts, of which at least all

[23] Gellhorn, *When Americans Complain*, p. 93.

but the national part would pose no barriers to the successful functioning of the Ombudsman.

As for the separation of powers, although many Americans see the doctrine as properly implemented only by their own governmental system, it is extremely difficult if not impossible to determine from general statements of the doctrine which forms of government satisfy its conditions and which do not. It can be argued that the cabinet, or parliamentary, governments of Europe satisfy them as well as American government, although Montesquieu, often mistakenly considered the father of the doctrine, would not have seen our form, and probably not the cabinet form either, as satisfying them. Indeed, all that can be said with certainty is that a single man or group making, executing, and judging the application of law would be a violation, and no modern democratic system approaches this situation.

Rather than attempt to determine whether or not the Ombudsman violates the separation of powers, we might consider whether the Ombudsman is compatible with or contributes to the goals of the doctrine. Historically, the five goals have been

1. To create greater governmental efficiency;
2. To assure that statutory law is made in the common interest;
3. To assure that the law is impartially administered and that all administrators are under the law;
4. To allow the people's representatives to call executive officials to account for the abuse of their power; and
5. To establish a balance of governmental powers.[24]

The Ombudsman clearly contributes to the achievement of the first three goals. While the fourth goal implies the impeachment procedure which is rarely used in the United States, it can be said that the Ombudsman's discovery of a grave abuse of power by an administrative official would lead to his being called to account in some manner. As for any balance which may exist among the legislative, executive, and judicial branches of government, it is difficult to see how the Ombudsman, an institution independent of the other branches in its operations and possessing only the power to recommend, could affect except in a salutary way the influence one branch might have over another.

What Americans often appear to have in mind when they speak of the separation of powers is not a normative doctrine very generally prescribing the governmental arrangements deemed necessary for achieving certain social goals, but some aspects of the relationship believed to exist among the branches of the federal and state govern-

[24] W. B. Gwyn, *The Meaning of the Separation of Powers* (New Orleans, 1965), pp. 127-128.

ments of the United States. Because the Ombudsman has not heretofore been added to governmental arrangements precisely like our own, some persons have suggested that it might prove incompatible with the American form of government with its separately elected and mutually independent executive and legislative branches and its independent judiciary.

As none of the proposals for an Ombudsman in America places the courts within its jurisdiction, the independence of the judiciary can hardly be undermined. The only effect an Ombudsman would have upon the American judiciary would be to receive some of the complaints which otherwise would be taken to court; however, it cannot be viewed as unsatisfactory if citizens are provided a channel of complaint in some circumstances preferable to the judicial channel. Since independent judiciaries of the American sort are found in the existing Ombudsman countries, this is an additional reason not to fear the Ombudsman's impact on the courts.

It is the American legislative-executive relations, usually seen as very different from those in Scandinavia and New Zealand, that cause the most apprehension about bringing the Ombudsman to the United States. It is alleged that while the Ombudsman works very well in cabinet systems, where the executive stays in office only with the support of the elected legislature, it would not work in the presidential system with its mutually independent and frequently disagreeing executive and legislature. Actually, as Professor Stanley V. Anderson has pointed out, the five countries with successfully operating Ombudsmen by no means have identical forms of government and one, Finland, has a government with both cabinet and presidential characteristics.[25] We have already observed that the very nature of the Ombudsman makes it unlikely that it will affect the power relations among existing governmental structures. In the countries in which it has been adopted there is no evidence that these relations have been affected. Indeed, an important basis for optimism about the transferability of the Ombudsman is that it fits easily into a variety of democratic governmental settings.

One problem of placing the Ombudsman in an American setting, which has caused unnecessary concern, has been the method of his appointment. Some of the proposals for this country provide for appointment by the chief executive with some form of legislative consent. Others, however, have rejected this traditional method of appointment, in the belief that it would give the executive too much control over the Ombudsman. Certainly if the traditional American method of appointment would allow the chief executive to determine the de-

[25] Stanley V. Anderson, "Connecticut Ombudsman?," *Case and Comment* (March-April, 1965), 4-6.

cisions of the Ombudsman, it should be rejected. It does not appear, however, that such appointment in itself gives the chief executive great influence over the activities of office holders. The President of the United States, for example, has not controlled the decisions of federal judges or the Comptroller General. The American method of appointment does open the possibility of undue executive influence since a person in office may be hesitant to incur the wrath of the chief executive who later may not propose him for reappointment. While it is probably unlikely that an Ombudsman would thus offend a chief executive, the independence and impartiality of the Ombudsman could be guaranteed by giving him a single term of, say, ten or twelve years.

PROBLEMS OF AMERICAN CULTURE

Although the cultural milieu of the United States is generally similar to that in Scandinavia and New Zealand, there are certain parts of the country where lack of consensus on perceptions and norms could diminish the effectiveness of a state or local Ombudsman. One would not be surprised to find the recommendations of Ombudsmen concerning the treatment of minority groups ignored by administrators and legislators alike. Supporters of Negro civil rights who see the Ombudsman as a means for combating discrimination probably will be disappointed. Even should an Ombudsman prevent racial discrimination, it is doubtful whether he can contribute significantly to reducing racial disturbances, for they are the result of far more than bureaucratic discrimination and poor Negroes may not find much security anyway in an official seen as another part of the "white power structure." In some cases, administrative abuses may be difficult for the Ombudsman to eradicate because they are strongly supported by the values and norms of administrators which find at least ambivalent support in society. This may be the case with "police brutality," which has been explained as the product of the policeman's outlook as it is determined by the nature of his occupation and the societal values of self initiative and the maintenance of order. To change this outlook, which leads to excessive and illegal violence against persons suspected of crimes, will require changing not only current police norms but also putting an end to the support given to them by such representatives of the community as grand juries, newspapers, and public officials, who are more frequently concerned with police efficiency than with the fair treatment of suspects.[26]

To mention these areas where the Ombudsman may not be effective in the United States is to remind ourselves that he is not a panacea

[26] Jerome H. Skolnick, *Justice Without Trial: Law Enforcement in a Democratic Society* (New York, 1966).

for all of the ills of society and especially not for the major ones. Only if it can be shown that American culture would seriously weaken the Ombudsman in handling all or most cases coming before him would there be reason to conclude that the institution would be of little or no use in the United States. It is sometimes maintained that it is all but impossible to keep party politics out of any institution in this country and that consequently there is great danger of the Ombudsman becoming a partisan figure, which would reduce his effectiveness considerably. Although a number of examples can be found of formally nonpartisan officials and institutions performing in a partisan manner, we should not be led to conclude that this is inevitably the case, for there are notable examples—the higher federal and state courts—which rarely if ever make partisan decisions. It is not unrealistic to predict that legal safeguards and public opinion will be able to keep an institution such as the Ombudsman free from political party pressures.

PROBLEMS OF OPPOSITION TO ADOPTION

The Ombudsman has been viewed favorably by persons and organizations from most parts of the American political spectrum, ranging from Mr. William F. Buckley and the American Bar Association Journal to the United Automobile Workers and Mr. Roy Wilkins of the NAACP. At the same time, no well known persons in this country have publicly declared themselves strongly against it. The vast majority of the American people are without a doubt unaware that the adoption of an Ombudsman has become a political issue, and of those who are aware probably most are not very concerned about it. This is what one would expect in the case of an unspectacular and relatively minor governmental reform. The same pattern occurred in other countries into which the Ombudsman has been introduced in recent years.

What groups, then, are ranged against the Ombudsman? One might expect civil servants and chief executives to be apprehensive, but there is no evidence to indicate that they are at present an important source of opposition to the Ombudsman. Instead, the strongest opposition appears to come from the members of the nation's legislative assemblies, who are fearful of losing what they believe to be an extremely important means for gathering and maintaining electoral support.

Because legislative support is essential for the adoption of the Ombudsman, an effort has been made to modify the institution in a way so as to remove the antagonism of legislators. It is primarily for this reason that Congressman Henry S. Reuss's proposal for a federal Ombudsman (H.R. 3388, 1967) provides that all citizens' complaints against administration can come to the Administrative Counsel of the

Congress, as he is called, only through Members of Congress. This is a relationship like that of the Parliamentary Commissioner and Members of Parliament in the United Kingdom, described in Chapter 1. The plan is supposed to appeal to legislators who will find their case work undiminished and at the same time receive expert assistance in handling it. In addition, it is intended to keep the case load of the Administrative Counsel within manageable limits.

Is the United States fated to have an incomplete Ombudsman or none at all? Before bowing before what some persons take to be the inevitable, advocates of the Ombudsman might try to allay the extravagant fears that many legislators seem to have of the institution. Legislators who believe that the Ombudsman will take away from them most of their case work are clearly wrong. If Professor Gellhorn's sampling of Congressional case work is any indication of the true state of affairs, only a small part of it—probably an average of 10 or 15 per cent—is concerned with complaints against administration, the rest being related to requests for information and for assistance in getting jobs or special privileges from the government. Even if an Ombudsman received every one of the complaints against administration, it appears that legislators would continue to have plenty of opportunities to build electoral support through case work. But there is no reason to believe that all such complaints would go to the Ombudsman. Although neither the Ombudsman's friends or foes mention it, one of the greatest threats to the successful operation of the Ombudsman in the United States may well be the habit of many American people to turn to their legislative representatives with complaints about administration, a habit reinforced by the belief that the political power of the legislator will give them a special advantage in the encounters with government bureaucracy. There is every reason to believe that if citizens are given direct access to an Ombudsman they nevertheless will continue to take many of their complaints to their legislative representatives. This, for example, has been the case in New Zealand. Mr. Larry Hill, an American political scientist who has carried on intensive research into the operations of the Ombudsman there, has reported that "most Ombudsman-type complaints still go to the M.P. and from him to the Minister." In a very few instances the legislators have sent complaints to the Ombudsman to handle. It is the opinion of informed persons in New Zealand that the Ombudsman's presence has caused no drop in legislative case loads, and some go so far as to say that the publicity concerning the Ombudsman has so increased public awareness of the possibility of appeals against administrative abuses and mistakes as to actually increase the loads.[27]

[27] Letter to the author dated August 27, 1967.

PROBLEMS OF THE FORMATIVE YEARS

Whether the Ombudsman has been transferred successfully to the United States will not be known until a few years after its formal adoption, when the pattern of interrelated activities which constitute its structure is seen to be stable and when the desirable consequences of the institution are seen to flow from these activities. The establishment of the pattern depends, of course, on a good deal more than simply the legal provisions creating the institution. It will be necessary to bring the advantages of the Ombudsman to the attention of the public, and this will require publicity in the mass media including an energetic campaign by the first Ombudsman to create public awareness and respect. Perhaps the most important requirement is proper selection of the first Ombudsman. A special effort should be made to keep party considerations as much as possible out of the initial appointment in order to establish the precedent of non-partisan choice. Even more essential is the choice of an exceptionally well qualified person, for the first Ombudsman probably will have an influence on the office long outlasting his own tenure.

The first occupant of the Ombudsman's office will create a role which, if accepted by the public and the groups with which he is most closely related, will provide a standard of conduct for future occupants. It is vital that the first occupant clearly understand the character of his office and the environmental conditions in which he will operate. As he will not have an established role to step into, he should be a creative, imaginative person, possessing at the same time a strong sense of the politically possible to guard him in the absence of an established role against the dangers of attempting too much or too little. As he will take a large part in making citizens aware of and confident in the Ombudsman's office, he should be an enthusiastic and convincing proselytizer. In addition to these special attributes the first occupant should have those of any successful Ombudsman. Dealing constantly with bureaucrats and legal problems, he should have considerable experience with public administration and training in the law. Possessed only with the power to advise, he should be especially persuasive and tactful. The greater the extent the first Ombudsmen in the United States possess these ideal characteristics, the greater the chances for the institution's success. The examples of the Danish, Norwegian, and New Zealand Ombudsmen show that the quest for close approximations of the ideal is not quixotic.

John E. Moore

3

State Government and the Ombudsman

The numerous proposals described elsewhere in this volume bear witness to the increasing visibility of the Ombudsman concept among state legislators; its inclusion in *Time* Magazine's annual quiz for students of public affairs confirms its recognition by the media; and, its use as an advertising gimmick in California newspapers indicates the versatility of the term, if not the concept. Indeed, as Professor Rowat observes, the word is being used so freely that it has begun to lose its precision. Why this sudden vogue in the United States? Does it indicate a genuine need for more sophisticated treatment of specific ills, or does it simply reflect the hypochondria of the body politic, continuing its search for some nostrum to combat that ache-all-over feeling attributed to bureaucracy? What sort of relief do we seek, and what alternative remedies are available?

The Need For Data

Chapter 2 offers a theoretical analysis of Ombudsman's prospects in this country, and some comparisons with alternative means of achieving related objectives. While the feasibility of transferring Ombudsman to the United States may remain a matter of informed conjecture until the attempt has been made, judgments of its desirability incorporate certain assumptions which are capable of empirical verification. Whether or not Ombudsman affords a worthy means of achieving stipulated goals remains a legitimate question.

JOHN E. MOORE *is Assistant Professor of Political Science at the University of California in Santa Barbara. Previously on the staff of the Brookings Institution, he received his A.B. from Reed College and his Ph.D. from Princeton University.*

It should not be obscured by unsubstantiated claims regarding the capacity of existing institutions to perform the central functions attributed to Ombudsman.

This essay will be primarily concerned with the collection and analysis of data required to evaluate the performance and potential of presently available channels of redress and oversight. Our principal laboratory will be the state of California; our objective to improve the quality of debate over the desirability of establishing an Ombudsman at the state level. We will be concerned with three central questions: (1) what do advocates of state Ombudsmen hope to achieve? (2) to what extent are their objectives attainable through existing public instrumentalities?; and (3) is the gap sufficient to require some form of institutional innovation?

The "desirable consequences" generally attributed to the office of Ombudsman are described in Chapter 2. Professor Gwyn's catalog embraces most of the objectives cited by sponsors of state Ombudsman, including (in roughly descending order of priority): (1) redress of individual grievances; (2) collective protection against improper and inefficient administration; (3) increased public confidence in administration, and reduced citizen alienation from a burgeoning and increasingly remote government; (4) improved performance of legislative functions through provision of continuous oversight, through identification of recurring problems which may require corrective legislation, and through alleviation of the complaint-handling burden presently borne by individual legislators and their staff; (5) protection of civil servants against unfounded criticism, contributing in turn to the improvement of their morale. Interrelated with these objectives are certain attributes of the instrumentality through which they are to be achieved, including accessability, impartiality, expertise, uniform treatment, and reliance upon informal sanctions.

Appraisals of the extent to which the preceding objectives and conditions are met by existing mechanisms will of course vary from one state to another. But the utility of Ombudsman as a corrective for any deficiencies which may be found will not vary directly with the extent of those deficiencies. Where, for example, members of the state legislature are so starved for staff assistance that complaint-handling is treated as a third or fourth order priority, it would be easy to make a case for Ombudsman. However, it may be argued that staff increases contributing more directly to improvement of law-making as well as complaint-handling functions would be more useful than creation of an Ombudsman. Moreover, the same conditions responsible for the shortcomings of existing institutions may present major obstacles to the establishment of an effectively functioning Ombudsman. Conversely, those states which appear to be doing a reasonably good job of performing many of the functions attributed to Ombudsman may experience greater demand for expansion of these functions, may be more receptive to the proposal, and may be able to make more effective use of the office once established. This is not to suggest that a choice must be made between improvement of existing mechanisms and creation of an Ombudsman, but to stress the note of caution implicit in the maxim that Ombudsman may be most effective where seemingly least needed. No toting up of black marks against a given state will provide an automatic index of its need for Ombudsman.

For reasons of convenience, necessity, and scholarly purpose our analysis focuses on the state of California. The maturity and comparatively generous staffing of both the Legislature and Governor's office guards against any temptation to make an easy case based upon the surface deficiencies noted above, as one might by using, say, Nevada. Since we are primarily concerned with empirical verification of assumptions regarding the adequacy of conventional public instruments for the redress of grievances and improvement of administration, the availability of data is critical, and pilot studies have been completed in California under the auspices of U. C. Berkeley's Institute of Governmental Studies. Finally, Ombudsman is a live issue in California. Assembly Speaker Jesse Unruh's bill has twice cleared the lower house, focusing attention and eliciting commentary on related but ordinarily submerged activities in the Legislature, Governor's office, and executive agencies.

We will conclude this brief summary of the intent and scope of the essay by specifying certain alternatives to Ombudsman which will *not* be considered here: (1) private channels of redress—such as "action lines" and the ACLU—because their availability is too unpredictable to provide a reliable means of achieving public policy goals, their inquiries lack the force implicit in a statutory or political mandate, and they fail to contribute to the general improvement of administrative organization and procedure; (2) courts and law officers of the state, as their capacity to perform Ombudsman-like functions is critically impaired by the cost to the complainant of pursuing judicial remedies, and by their limited jurisdiction; (3) intra-agency machinery for review or appeal, on grounds that it is in fact or appearance insufficiently objective to qualify as an alternative to Ombudsman.

Inclusion of the complaint-handling activities of the Governor's office may be considered marginal, to the extent that the objectivity of his staff is diminished by an inclination to discount complaints or criticism affecting the administration for which the Governor is ultimately responsible. However, we are not persuaded that the Governor's relationship to his administration is comparable to that of a director to his agency. The Governor's constituency is more inclusive, and his interest in forestalling an accumulation of grievances against his administration is likely to be greater than his concern for protecting the self-esteem of a particular agency. Moreover, it can be argued that while the popular election of certain state officials may reduce the Governor's ability to control their agencies, it may also increase his ability to provide objective treatment of complaints against them.

Analogous Institutions

Among the formal instrumentalities of the state, perhaps the closest analogy to Ombudsman is to be found in California's Commission on Judicial Qualifications, discussed at greater length in Chapter 5. Indeed, within its jurisdiction, certain of the Commission's activities are virtually indistinguishable from those associated with Ombudsman. The Commission was created with rather narrowly defined functions in view: to investigate and hold hearings on complaints alleging the misconduct, failure of performance, habitual intemperance, or disability of judges; to encourage the resignation or retirement of unfit judges, and—where necessary—to recommend that an order of removal be issued by the State Supreme Court. As originally conceived, the Commission's options were limited, in effect, to acquittal or recommended expulsion. The Commission's Executive Secretary has summarized its response to the void thus created:

> In the course of processing complaints and conducting investigations it became apparent that sometimes behavior and activities, while not warranting removal from office, were improper and subject to criticism. The process of investigating might include setting out a credible complaint in an interview with or a letter to a judge and asking for his comment and explanation. This often has the effect of correcting the alleged dereliction.[1]

In its efforts to correct the cause of complaint through measures which—at their most severe—entail recommendations to the California Supreme Court, the Commission exhibits most of the essential attributes of an Ombudsman: impartiality, expertise, and inability to impose direct sanctions. The only significant discrepancy relates to the Commission's accessability, which is for practical purposes limited to members of the bar. Since this limitation stems from public ignorance rather than statutory restraint, it could be corrected through publicity. The Commission and Ombudsman would seem to differ most perceptibly in their orientations. Where the Ombudsman is concerned primarily with the redress of individual grievances and secondarily with elimination of their source, the Commission is concerned almost

[1] Jack E. Frankel, Executive Secretary, California Commission on Judicial Qualifications, in testimony before the Interim Committee on Governmental Organization, California Legislative Assembly, Sept. 26, 1966 (p. 87).

exclusively with the target of complaints: "our investigation [is con-
ducted] in such a way as to see if some action should be taken
against the judge, not whether something should be done on behalf of
some individual." The complainant may benefit in the immediate
case or in future cases before the same judge; his grievance will be
considered and possibly redressed, but from the Commission's viewpoint the particular result is of secondary importance. California's
innovative Commission on Judicial Qualifications is being emulated in
other states. Where available, this device provides an effective substitute for Ombudsman in handling complaints within its jurisdiction.

More extensive in scope but less effective in operation are the
provisions in many states for publication of administrative rules and
regulations, and—in a smaller number of states—for the oversight of
administrative procedures. Publication requirements are a *sine qua
non* of responsible government; they do not in themselves assure the
equity of the rule or of its particular application. Systematic clearance
of proposed rules and regulations promises an evaluation of their
compliance with procedural requirements, but only a quarter of the
states provide for such clearance (most commonly through the Attorney General's office), and its value depends on the quality of the
standards applied. While a few states provide for legislative review of
rules and regulations already in effect, it is frequently made per-
functory by the competition of more pressing responsibilities.

The potential of the preceding mechanisms should not be obscured
by the gap between intent and execution: this can be reduced through
more or less conventional organizational reforms. California has
established an independent Office of Administrative Procedure to enforce the requirements of its Administrative Procedure Act, and to
make continuing studies looking toward improvement of the administrative process. The critical shortcoming of these provisions for the
oversight of administrative procedure is not a function of their faulty
execution, but of their inability to reach individual grievances, or
actions which may be procedurally correct but unnecessarily injurious
in a particular case. As New Zealand's Ombudsman has pointed out,
efforts to standardize and enforce procedural requirements should
be regarded as corollaries of Ombudsman, rather than substitutes. They
would enable an Ombudsman to do his job more effectively, but they
are not suited to do the same job.

In addition to spotty provisions for oversight of administrative rules,
regulations and procedures through interim committees or legislative
councils, several states have equipped their legislatures with professionally staffed bureaus whose responsibilities include recommending
improvements of administrative organization and efficiency. The
prototype is California's Office of the Legislative Analyst. Invaluable

as a source of technical advice, these bureaus nevertheless suffer from most of the afflictions attributed to the legislature's committees. More immediate budgetary matters demand attention, and of the time spent on administrative improvement, little can be devoted to the comparatively expensive consideration of individual complaints. Perhaps the closest approximation of this central function of the Ombudsman has been achieved in the Wisconsin Legislature, where a joint interim committee hears complaints from individuals alleging injury from administrative procedures. Like Ombudsman, the committee's powers are advisory only, but its advice carries the weight of potential legislative action. According to the committee's executive secretary,

> I have known of cases where a mere warning to a department that the committee will hold a hearing on a certain matter if the department does not act to change its procedures has resulted in the desired action. In other cases the department has satisfied the committee that statutory authority is inadequate to permit the desired action and legislation has been introduced to permit it. In a few cases the committee has sponsored legislation to force the department to act in the desired way.[2]

The committee's effectiveness as an alternative to Ombudsman is presently impaired by the paucity of complaints received, but these and certain other defects might be corrected by conventional remedies. Given increased accessibility, adequate staff support, and a warrant to look beyond questions of procedural correctness, the committee's experience suggests the possibility of achieving the objectives thought to be served by Ombudsman through reform of existing instrumentalities. It should be emphasized, however, that as presently constituted the joint interim committee does not achieve those objectives, and would be enabled to do so only by grafting on the essential attributes of Ombudsman. Moreover, the committee's potential might still be limited by its direct connection with the Legislature through overlapping membership. Lacking effective insulation from the Legislature, the committee might be used as a vehicle for embarrassing the administration, and the mere suggestion of bias could dissipate that aura of impartiality which has helped Ombudsman to secure the cooperation of administrative personnel.

With the exception of California's Commission on Judicial Qualifications, the formal instrumentalities of state government appear to offer little promise of achieving the goals associated with Ombudsman, even if their potential is fully realized. Legislative oversight committees and service agencies are faced with competing responsibilities, and within the time and effort which can be devoted to improving admin-

---

[2] Quoted in a Report of the Alaska Legislative Council, *Legislative Oversight of the Administration of Statutes* (1964), p. 42.

istration, must give priority to general rules and procedures. Where particular grievances are considered—as in the case of Wisconsin's joint interim committee—accessibility and staff assistance are limited, and the committee's impartiality may be questioned. The Commission on Judicial Qualifications is weakened only by its limited accessibility, but because of its specialized jurisdiction must be regarded as an auxiliary rather than an alternative device.

Although the formal machinery of the state appears to be equipped —at best—to handle general problems of administrative organization, procedure and efficiency, it may still be argued that the particular problems of individuals can be resolved within the informal channels of redress provided by the Governor's office and the Legislature. Together with intimidating predictions of cost and bureaucratic megalomania, the assumed efficacy of complaint-handling by elected representatives is one of the major weapons in the arsenal of Ombudsman's critics. Like the deterrent effect alleged by advocates of Ombudsman, the assumption is untested; unlike the deterrent effect, the complaint-handling capabilities of elected repesentatives can be measured without resort to elaborate methodological contrivances. Where the effectiveness of prevention must be evaluated in terms of things that do not happen, the effectiveness of elective complaint-handling involves things that *do* happen. Since the assumption that the job is already being done has a critical bearing on the desirability of introducing Ombudsman to state government, failure to verify it must be attributed to lethargy, lack of financial support, or fear that analysis will discredit either the assumption or its critics.

Informal Complaint-handling Activities

In May of 1965, the Legislative Reference Service published a survey of the literature on case work by members of Congress. It begins as follows:

> Many books and articles on Congress—especially those dealing with the duties of Congressmen—mention so-called case work performed by Members. Unfortunately, the subject is seldom treated in detail or approached in any systematic fashion. Journalists, academicians, and even Members themselves (although the latter are usually more informative) tend to deal with the matter in terms of unique or vague statistics, anecdotes, polemics, and/or justification.[3]

Insofar as Congress is concerned, the situation has improved somewhat since completion of the survey. In their study of congressional

[3] Walter Kravitz, *Case Work by Members of Congress: Analysis Based on a Survey of Existing Literature*, the Library of Congress, Legislative Reference Service (Washington: mimeo, May 4, 1965), p. 1.

reform, Professors Davidson, Kovenock and O'Leary utilized a random sample of 87 members of the House of Representatives to obtain a more accurate cross-section of the congressman's perception of his work and problems, including constituent service.[4] Professor Gellhorn's *When Americans Complain* incorporates his analysis of a random sampling of the mail going in and out of ten congressional offices. While this investigation does not aspire to comprehensiveness, it does provide a more reliable indication of the volume and composition of congressional mail than was previously available. In 1965 a literature on casework had to be synthesized from peripheral sources, most commonly works concerned with the duties of congressmen or with congressional reform. That literature has now been enriched by at least two studies integrating original data and secondary materials in a focused appraisal of the complaint-handling capabilities of Congress: Chapter II of the Gellhorn book ("Watchmen in Washington"), and Kenneth Olson's evaluation of "The Service Function of the United States Congress." [5]

Although the literature on Congress lacks statistical accuracy and frequently suffers from imprecision, it is rapidly improving. Unfortunately, even the grim picture painted by the Legislative Reference Service might be considered an empiricist's paradise by students of complaint-handling in state legislatures. Here one surveys a virtual wasteland, brightened only by a few pages in the Wahlke, Eulau, *et al.*, study of *The Legislative System*, an incisive commentary by the ubiquitous Walter Gellhorn in Chapter III of *When Americans Complain*, and Dean Mann's study of complaint-handling by state legislators in California, cited below.

If our objective is to evaluate the efficacy of informal complaint-handling procedures, what do we need to know? What kinds of information should be encompassed in an outline for systematic data collection? With regard to the complaint-handling activities of the members, committees, and service agencies of the state legislature, we might begin by collating data on variations among the states relating to the following two categories:

1. expectations regarding the extent of the state legislator's responsibilities, for which rough indices may be found in the frequency and length of legislative sessions, and rates of compensation. We may assume that legislative activity is not considered a full-time job where

---

[4] See U.S. Congress, Joint Committee on the Organization of Congress, *Hearings Pursuant to S. Con. Res. 2*, 89th Congress, 1st session, Washington, D.C., 1965, p. 775, and Roger Davidson, David Kovenock, and Michael O'Leary, *Congress in Crisis: Politics and Congressional Reform* (Belmont, Calif.: Wadsworth, 1966), p. 77.

[5] Alfred de Grazia, ed., *Congress: The First Branch of Government* (Washington, D.C.: American Enterprise Institute for Public Policy Research, 1966).

the legislature meets briefly every other year, and where annual compensation—if an exclusive source of income—would qualify the recipient for welfare assistance.

2. the level of staff support relevant to the performance of complaint-handling functions, including the nature and availability of centralized service agencies, and the provision of staff assistance for individual legislators.

Some of the above information can be gleaned from such readily available sources as *The Book of the States,* but it permits nothing more than crude inferences (e.g., that a legislator who assumes the role for 60 days in alternate years, receives a token stipend, and lacks personal staff assistance may not be visible enough to attract many complaints, will not have much incentive to pursue the complaints he does receive, and will not be equipped to deal with them effectively even if he should be inclined to try). The data would at best perform an exclusionary function, indicating those states in which the legislature cannot even aspire to provide a significant vehicle for handling complaints. More refined measures of responsibility and support are required to embrace the remaining states, and these must be accompanied by data of the sort that is just beginning to emerge from the literature on Congressional case work, relating to the following five categories:

1. The legislator's role concept. Is constituent service regarded as a significant and meritorious activity? A comparison of excerpts from Wahlke's *The Legislative System* and Gellhorn's *When Americans Complain* suggests the possibility of significant variations among the states, and also indicates the hazards of extrapolating from a limited sample.

> Of the 474 legislators interviewed in the four states [California, New Jersey, Ohio and Tennessee], only 27 per cent spontaneously mentioned what one may call "service functions" as important aspects of their legislative job, and not all of these functions are in the nature of "service," literally interpreted. (Wahlke, et. al., p. 304.)

> When they [Massachusetts legislators] were asked "which, of all the things you are called on to do, do you think is most important to the people of your district?" by far the largest single number answered "help with individual problems, personal favors, listening to problems, being available, 'attending to their needs' "—and the number would have been still greater had not some of the respondents chosen particular subheadings such as "information," "jobs," "making contacts," "pensions," "veterans' problems," and "service." (Gellhorn, p. 136, Fn. 10.)

2. The nature, sources, and volume of complaints. What is the characteristic "mix," in terms of breadth, complexity, and variety? To what extent do complainants seek policy changes which the legislator may

not be able or willing to accomplish, but clearly fall within his competence as a legislator? To what extent do they seek accelerated actions which the legislator is not competent to evaluate in terms of merit, but which are easily disposed of, by both the legislator and the bureaucrat to whom they are relayed? To what extent do they seek a different result in an administrative action so complex that the legislator can evaluate neither the merit of the complaint nor the justice of the agency's response? Do complaints tend to cluster around a limited number of functions or agencies, enabling the legislator or his staff to develop a measure of expertise? In brief, we need data permitting a qualitative assessment of the legislator's dependence on the target agencies—that is, the administrative agencies at which complaints are aimed.

With a state Ombudsman in view as an alternative, it would also be useful to know (1) what percentage of complaints involve federal or local agencies, and (2) how the state legislator responds to these misdirected complaints. Does he ignore jurisdictional boundaries and contact federal or local agencies directly, does he develop informal referral arrangements with legislators at other levels of government, or does he simply return the complaint with a suggestion that the complainant seek relief within the appropriate jurisdiction?

Does the nature or volume of complaints vary significantly with the composition of the legislator's constituency? What are the distinguishing variables—the size of the district; the density and the stability of its population; its predominant socio-economic patterns, degree of urbanization, etc.? Does the legislator receive a disproportionately small number of complaints from members of the opposite party? Many of these queries should be addressed to variations among states as well as within them.

3. The complaint-handling activities of the legislator's personal staff, the professional staff attached to legislative committees, and the legislature's centralized service agencies. Referring solely to a state legislator's ability to process complaints—to do *something*, regardless of the ultimate benefit to the complainant or contribution to improved administration—it has been argued that it would be easier to expand the capacity of his staff than to reduce its burden by establishing an Ombudsman.

How much time is devoted to handling constituent complaints, by the legislator and his staff? With what other activities does complaint-handling compete, and how often does it yield? How rapidly and thoroughly does the staff look into complaints? How carefully does the legislator supervise their case work? (Since his secretary never indicated that she was unable to keep up with the flow of mail, one California Assemblyman assumed that he was taking good care of his constituents' complaints. When she resigned, her replacement discovered a file drawer stuffed full of unanswered complaints.)

In most states, provision of professional staff assistance to legislative committees is inadequate for the more obvious purposes of arranging hearings, conducting research, and assisting in the formulation of policy alternatives, let alone investigating individual complaints. But a professional committee staff might combine the Ombudsmanic virtues of expertise, objectivity, and ability to identify patterns of complaints indicating corrective legislation. Where their jurisdictions encompass functions likely to occasion complaints from individuals (e.g., social welfare, public health, education), what role is played by the committee staff in responding to these grievances? In what number and from what sources are complaints directed to the committee staff? Since they possess similar attributes, it would be useful to make the same inquiries regarding the central service agencies—what is their potential for handling individual complaints, and how extensively are they used for this purpose?

4. The impact of legislative intercession, and perceptions of the functions performed. What actually happens when an individual complains to his state legislator? What proportion of the complaints received are pursued? In what percentage of cases is administrative action (1) unaffected or possibly delayed; (2) accelerated; (3) reversed or significantly altered?

What do the participants *believe* is accomplished by legislative intervention? (1) From the viewpoint of the complainant, is the legislator's sympathetic attention valued in itself, or only when it leads to a favorable result? (2) What does the legislator think he is doing for his constituent, for himself (as a legislator and as a prospective candidate for reelection), and for the administrative agencies he contacts? (3) Does the administrator perceive legislative inquiries as simply meddlesome, or as affording a source of additional information, an opportunity to justify particular actions through an "impartial" intermediary, an occasion for raising more general problems regarding the agency's appropriation or statutory mandate?

5. The factors which enable the legislator to get results. Where his intercession contributes to prompter action or a different outcome, what are the key variables—fuller information? errors revealed in the closer scrutiny prompted by a legislator's inquiry? precedents overlooked or more generous options invoked in an effort to please him? formal requirements bent in proportion to his perceived ability to affect the agency's fortunes in the legislature?

For the most part, the preceding outline seeks data relating to activities and outcomes for which analogies can be found in the literature on congressional case work. There is, however, no corresponding literature at the national level for the role played by the Governor's office in treating citizen complaints. As previously noted, the Governor's office may not appear to provide an impartial channel of redress for grievances occasioned by "his" administration. Yet one of the most common criticisms of state government relates to the Governor's lack of authority over administrative agencies. We know something about his weakness as a chief administrator, but virtually nothing about his performance or potential as a complaint-handler.

Rather then rehearse a full catalog of queries which would frequently duplicate the preceding one, we will simply indicate a few variations on its major themes. We need information regarding: (1) the extent, use and organization of the Governor's staff for purposes of handling citizen complaints; (2) the attitudes of his offce toward these complaints—are they perceived as implied rebukes, as opportunities to forestall an accumulation of grievances which might prove costly at the polls, or as means of spot-checking the performance of administrative agencies for which the Governor is ostensibly responsible? (3) the nature and volume of complaints directed to the Governor's office, the extent to which that volume varies according to the prominence of the legislature, and the extent to which the Governor's office depends upon or scrutinizes agency responses; (4) the impact of inquiries issuing from the Governor's office, and the factors contributing to or impairing their effectiveness; (5) the central functions which the participants believe are served through intercession by the Governor's office.

In many of these categories, comparions of data on the legislature and Governor's office should prove instructive. For example, it is sometimes claimed that an Ombudsman would simply provide another means of relaying the same complaint to the same agency. This criticism suffers from its neglect of the expertise, impartiality, and focus which a proper Ombudsman would provide, but it nevertheless raises some significant questions. Are complaints directed to state legislators or to the Governor in a random fashion? Or are patterns of preselection discernible—the Governor receiving more petitions from prison inmates, the legislator more complaints from aggrieved motorists? Would additional channels duplicate the present flow of complaint mail, divert it from one channel to another, or tap new sources? Comparisons of the composition of complaint mail received by the Governor and state legislators should provide better clues, if not authoritative answers.

The very dimensions of our outline indicate how little we presently know about informal means of grievance redress in state government, and how poorly equipped we are to argue the merits of Ombudsman

in the absence of fuller knowledge regarding the adequacy of existing machinery. Given the data specified above, it should be possible to
(1) evaluate the performance of conventional devices at the state
level; (2) sharpen projections of their potential; (3) make informed
comparisons with the potential of Ombudsman in this country, and
(4) in conjunction with state-by-state political analyses, evaluate the
comparative utility of Ombudsman and alternative means of improving complaint-handling capabilities. This is an ambitious agenda. For
the time being we must be content with such inferences as can be
made on the basis of personal observation, a sparse and fragmentary
literature, and—most importantly—the pilot projects sponsored by the
University of California's Institute of Governmental Studies: Dean
Mann's *Complaint Handling by State Legislators*; and Gerald Mc-
Daniel's *Letters of Complaint:Mail-Processing in California's Administrative Branch.*

California's Experience: Some Improvisations

In the following pages we will suggest a few hypotheses
derived from the questions we have raised, drawing upon examples
and findings from the Institute projects. The limitations of this analysis
should be made clear:

1. Most of the supporting data relates to informal complaint-handling procedures in California, where both the Legislature and Gov-
erner enjoy comparatively lavish facilities and staff assistance.

2. Professor Mann's study is based upon information compiled by
three graduate students working in the offices of two Assemblymen
and one Senator during the summer of 1966. All of the legislators
were Democrats; one Assemblyman and one Senator represented overlapping constituencies—an agricultural area sprinkled with several
small cities—and the second Assemblyman an urban district in one of
California's major metropolitan centers. The study presents a unique
set of cases—it does not purport to offer a representative sample in
terms of party affiliations, the socioeconomic characteristics of the
districts involved, nor the flow and composition of complaint mail
throughout the year. Moreover, the investigators assisted in the handling of complaints, thereby (unavoidably) compounding their intru-
sion in the process they were observing.

3. With respect to the volume, composition and routing of mail
directed to the Governor's office, Professor McDaniel's tabulations
range from a comprehensive tally of agency referrals by the Correspondence Unit during the first six months of calendar 1965, to a
breakdown of mail leaving the Assistant Cabinet Secretary's office
during selected months in the spring of 1964. (Mail processed by the

Correspondence Unit accounts for 50 per cent or more of the total received, and involves more or less routine matters; mail handled in the office of the Assistant Cabinet Secretary is second in volume only to the Correspondence Unit, and involves the bulk of complaints not referred to staff secretaries with specialized jurisdictions.) The staff secretaries were interviewed regarding their complaint work, but uniform schedules were not employed. In addition to his compilation of data on mail-handling in the Governor's office, Professor McDaniel completed less rigorous studies of procedures and attitudes in the five most frequently affected administrative agencies, and gathered a sampling of attitudes toward Assembly Speaker Unruh's Ombudsman proposal. All of the data was obtained during the adminstration of a Democratic Governor, so it is impossible to make comparisons on the basis of partisan affiliation.

ATTITUDES TOWARD COMPLAINT WORK

Initially, Professor Mann's study did not undertake direct probes of the attitudes of legislators toward complaint-handling; it concentrated on the office as a whole, rather than the individual legislator. One result of this broader focus was to indicate the importance of distinguishing between the attitudes of the legislator and his staff. Subsequent interviews revealed that each of the legislators placed a high value on constituent service, viewing it as an integral part of the job and a political necessity. But in one office a staff assistant appeared to feel that constituent service "interfered" with more legitimate activities, and the intern in another office observed that

> the way in which complaints are handled, if they are handled at all, depends almost wholly upon the attitude of the administrative assistant. By the very nature of his position, an assistant is forced to consider political matters as being more important than constituent complaints. This means that during a time of great activity, such as election time, complaints are set aside for matters of "greater importance." . . . The attitude of the assistant is very important. He may easily set cases aside and the complaint will never be heard.

In response to a questionnaire distributed to administrative assistants of Democratic Assemblymen, those who replied indicated that they devoted more time to constituent service than to any other single activity, a mean of 32 per cent. Their corresponding estimate of time spent on constituent service by the legislator himself was 13 per cent. While the administrative assistant's attitude is of course irrelevant in states where such assistance is not provided, its absence could have an important bearing on the legislator's attitude toward complaint handling. Thus in making interstate comparisons, it may be useful to distinguish between estimates of the importance and value of constituent service. A legislator who feels compelled to spend 50 per cent of his own time on constituent service evidently considers it an important activity, but he may discount its value in comparison with time spent on legislative matters. Conversely, a legislator who finds it necessary to devote no more than 13 per cent of his own time to handling complaints may discount the importance of this activity, but express a more charitable estimate of its value. We might hypothesize that the value placed on complaint-handling in the offices of state legislators will vary inversely with the volume of complaints and proportionally to the time and staff available to process them.

Attitudes toward complaint-handling in the offices of California Legislators appear to differ considerably among districts, between offices representing essentially the same district in the upper and lower houses, and even between the legislator and his staff within the same office. The attitudes of affected members of the Governor's staff are less resistant to generalization. Professor McDaniel concludes that

> the staff generally regards the handling of complaint mail as a continuous claim on their limited time, one that imposes an extra activity above and beyond their assigned duties . . .
>
> Because such services require personal attention, staff secretaries are inclined to feel that they spend more time handling letters than they can readily spare from other responsibilities. On the other hand, they recognize an obligation to take time and trouble; they consider that a citizen's appeal to the Governor is often so vital to him, regardless of the real weight of the problem, that failure to handle the problem expeditiously might be harmful to the Governor's political and popular image. Staff secretaries are concerned for citizen complaints as individuals also. However, such consideration may be lessened by the pressure of numbers and the necessity of avoiding personal involvement in order to retain perspective and one's own mental balance.

The sheer volume of mail received in the Governor's office does suggest one important reason why complaint-handling tends to be viewed as an "extra" rather than an integral activity of his staff. The total flow runs between 1,000 and 2,000 pieces per day. Elaborate screening procedures have been developed to sift out the mail requiring an individual response, and only a fraction of this (no more than a third) seeks redress of specific grievances. Over 50 per cent of the total is routed to a central Correspondence Unit for standard replies or direct referrals to administrative agencies. But a substantial amount of mail remains to be handled by the five staff secretaries who deal with virtually all complaints. In order of volume, they include (1) the Assistant Cabinet Secretary, who is confronted with between 1,000 and 1,600 pieces per month, approximately 25 per cent of which contain complaints; (2) the Extradition and Executive Clemency Secretary, who receives 300 to 400 complaints each month from prison inmates and their relatives; (3) the Secretary for Education Matters, who handles between 200 and 800 letters per month, about 30 per cent containing complaints; (4) the Assistant to the Governor for Human Rights, who responds to an average of 60 complaints a month, and (5) the Secretary to the Governor's Cabinet, who receives less complaint mail than any of the above, but nevertheless spends from one to one-and-one-half hours each day answering it. It should be noted that the Governor's staff is expected to answer *all* communications to which some reply is indicated, which is not always the case in legislators' offices.

In addition to the disproportionate amount of time which he sees being consumed by complaints, the attitude of the staff secretary may be significantly influenced by the seeming ambiguity of his role. There is a direct link between the legislator and his constituent, and despite possible differences in their attitudes toward complaint work, there is a close identification between the legislator and his administrative assistant. The Governor's relationship to a much larger constituency is considerably less direct, and only the exceptional or vainglorious staff secretary could regard himself as the Governor's alter-ego. In the absence of close identification with his superior, where does the staff secretary look for a general rationalization of his complaint-handling responsibilities? McDaniel's study indicates that the answer may relate to the degree of program specialization: "it appears that better attention is given to complaint mail in staff offices with specialized subjects of concern, such as civil rights, labor, penal and educational affairs." However, it may again prove useful to distinguish between estimates of importance and value. The staff secretary responsible for a circumscribed subject matter may have a clearer incentive to attend to complaint mail, yet still discount its value relative to his other responsibilities:

> . . . the secretary [for Human Rights] sees his work primarily as fostering larger scale "affirmative" policies and actions. When he gets tied up with complaints that drag on and involve heavy correspondence, he feels that he is taking a great deal of time from other important activities. However, he recognizes that it is necessary to satisfy complaints as nearly as possible.

Finally, the attitudes of the Governor's staff secretaries may be affected by their limited ability to pursue the complaints they receive: "few staff persons are satisfied that they do the best possible job of following up complaints, and of checking on the way agencies respond to citizens. Aside from implied powers wielded by the staff secretaries as members of the Governor's office, the secretaries have little formal authority to investigate any lack of responsiveness evident in agency letters."

We might hypothesize that attitudes toward handling constituent complaints in the Governor's office are primarily a function of (1) their volume; (2) their perceived relevance to the staff member's central responsibilities (for the Governor's general image as well as his specific programs), and (3) the influence which can be exerted on the speed and quality of responses (assuming that the majority of complaints are referred to administrative agencies).

Judging from interviews conducted in five of the agencies most frequently complained about, some parallels may be found in the factors contributing to the attitudes of the Governor's staff and to those of his top administrative officers. Two of the five directors indicated an awareness of the Governor's stake in the handling of complaints:

> Because he is appointed to represent the Governor, the Director (of employment) maintains a close liason with the Governor's office and feels that he should be as responsive to complainants as the Governor would be . . .
>
> Sensitivity to public complaints is a quality the Director (of Motor Vehicles) seeks to instill in his staff members. He ascribed his own sensitivity in these matters to his earlier experience within the Governor's office. He further believed that, as the Governor's appointee, he was required to be responsive and to make every effort to put the Governor and his administration in a good light. Thus, all mail returning to the Governor goes to the Director for review, and all letters go out over his signature.

Attitudes in three agencies appeared to correspond closely with perceptions of the relevance of complaints to the agency's objectives, and of the interests of its clientele: in Social Welfare, "it is the complaints we don't get that bother us most;" in Employment, the Director's primary concern "relates to complaints about services and attitude, or lack of courtesy by those administering services in the Department." Conversely, the Director of Professional and Vocational Standards indicated that

> . . . he feels no responsibility for bringing a license holder into line as the result of a legitimate complaint, nor does he feel that he should urge the agency or board to bring pressure on persons complained against. He pointed out that professional and vocational associations work very closely with the state boards that handle licensing. Board appointments conform to the wishes of the associations, and the fees charged to licensees are used to support the disciplining bodies.

Our hypothesis is that department heads will value complaint-handling in proportion to (1) their sense of responsibility to the Governor, and (2) the relevance of complaints to the agency's central mission and the interests of its predominant clientele.

THE NATURE, SOURCES, AND VOLUME OF COMPLAINTS

The subject matter of complaints might be arrayed along a continuum marked at one extreme by general policy concerns, and at the other by personal grievances resulting from the manner in which policy has been applied in a particular case. In the center would be the many ambiguous cases in which criticism of general policy is interrelated with a specific complaint. Of the 81 cases included in Professor Mann's study, 43 per cent involved complaints of unfair, discriminatory, or dilatory treatment; 32 per cent expressed concern with policies which had no direct bearing on the complainant's personal fortunes, and 25 per cent combined personal grievance with criticism of the policy from which it derived. Comparable figures are not available for mail directed to the Governor's office, but here are some illustrative cases drawn from both studies.

Specific Applications—A man came to the legislator's office for help in obtaining his disability check. He had filed the necessary forms, but had not received his check. He had also appealed his case to the Workmen's Compensation Board and to the Labor Commissioner. A phone call to the district office of the Disability Insurance Agency revealed that the complainant had filed somewhat later than he had indicated, and that he had filled out one form incorrectly, thereby delaying his claim. His case was further complicated by the fact that because he had filed with the other two state agencies, several additional actions were required before he could receive benefits. Nevertheless, the agency official indicated that his office was sending the disability check that very day. It appeared that the complainant was constantly involved in labor disputes and was well known to agency personnel.

A man expressed disapproval over the length of time required to register his wife's car. Since there had been some confusion regarding her name on the renewal slip, the Department of Motor Vehicles had requested the ownership certificate. He had sent this to the Department, but had not received the automobile registration after several weeks had elapsed. The legislator wrote to the Director, who responded that the corrections had been made and the validation sticker had been mailed. He indicated that although the problem had been handled correctly, there had been some delay owing to a heavy work load.

* * *

A letter of recommendation was written on behalf of an applicant for a state civil service position. The applicant passed his exams, but was rejected, allegedly over a "trifling technicality." The writer feels the rejection was due to the applicant's prior prison record, a factor he feels should not be considered in view of the applicant's excellent record since then. He requests [of the Governor] that the case be reviewed.

A Colorado businessman received jaywalking tickets on a business trip to California. He has since received a notice that due to nonpayment of fines a warrant has been issued and will be served should he return to California. The writer argues that he paid all fines, encloses photocopies of checks mailed, and asks the Governor to "clean up mess."

Policies per se—A letter was written to the legislator's office expressing concern for the health of the community. The correspondents said that a recent County Health Department sanitation report indicated that 383 eating establishments and 167 food markets in the county had not been inspected during the previous year. A phone call to the county health officer revealed that owing to a lack of personnel, the Department had not inspected all eating establishments and food markets in the county. There were three vacancies on the staff; low salaries had failed to attract applicants. In the previous four years there had been 13 resignations because of inadequate salaries. The county health officer felt that a 15 per cent salary increase was necessary to fill these positions. The legislator wrote to the complainants, thanking them for their concern, transmitting the information from the county health officer, and informing them that he would bring the matter to the attention of the Board of Supervisors. The legislator subsequently wrote to the Chairman of the Board of Supervisors recounting the constituents' complaint and expressing his view that the topic deserved consideration by the Board.

*   *   *

The Governor is urged to delay annexation of land by a city because the writer fears the kind of land development (apartment houses) that will take place.

The state should purchase a nearby hot spring in order to preserve it.

A proposed purchase of land at Malibu is opposed.

Policy Through Personal Grievances—A fairly typical case involving policy questions concerned a woman who complained about the Education Code with regard to nonresident tuition fees for college education. Although her son had been living in California, the parents' legal residence was in Colorado. The son would soon become 21 and would declare California his legal residence. In order to be classified as a resident student, he was required to maintain a one-year legal residence in California after his 21st birthday. Therefore, he would have to pay out-of-state tuition fees for the first school year. A call to the consultant to a legislative education committee indicated that these requirements would have to be met. The consultant indicated, however, that it was possible to obtain a waiver of out-of-state tuition fees in cases of financial need. He also suggested the possibility of obtaining a state loan. The woman expressed satisfaction with this information and with the legislator's efforts, and indicated that she would look into the possibilities.

*   *   *

The writer is having trouble renting a parcel of land because it is common knowledge that the state intends to purchase it eventually for a freeway. He requests reimbursement by the state for the rental he feels he should be getting.

Because of personal experience, the writer wants the Governor to appoint a special committee to investigate means of expediting civil cases.

The preceding cases indicate a significant relationship between the subject-matter of complaints and the complaint-handling ability of both state legislators and of the Governor's staff. In dealing with specific complaints alleging maladministration, the legislator and the Governor's staff secretary are almost entirely dependent upon the target agency for both information and policy explication. Barring a time-consuming independent investigation, how could the legislator determine whether or not the complainant seeking his disability check had filed timely and correct applications, or the Governor's staff secretary determine whether or not the civil service applicant's prison record had contributed to his rejection?

One of the legislators interviewed by Professor Mann remarked that the information supplied with 75 per cent of the complaints he received was inadequate, and in a substantial number of cases, misleading. The alternatives he perceived were to invest staff time in an effort to substantiate the allegation, or to waste it pursuing what might prove to be a clearly unjustified complaint. Since his office received no more than half-a-dozen complaints per week, independent verification was a meaningful alternative; it is not meaningful to the legislator who receives 50 to 100 complaints a week (as some California legislators do), nor to the gubernatorial staff secretary who is required to process between 60 and 100 complaints during the same period. As we have previously noted, the staff secretary's dependence upon the administrative agencies stems primarily from the breadth of his responsibilities and the shallowness of his formal powers. It should be pointed out that in four of the agencies to which complaints are most frequently referred by the Governor's office, the directors' influence is similarly attenuated by extensive decentralization of responsibility.

Although relevant to complaint-handling capabilities, dependence upon the target agency may not be debilitating where the alleged abuse involves dilatory actions (as with the Department of Motor Vehicles, above), or faulty records (as in the complaint to the Governor from the Colorado businessman). And dependence upon administrative agencies does not directly impair the legislator's competence in dealing with general policy matters, or with the policy implications of specific grievances. Although the DMV case involved a personal complaint, it may have sensitized the legislator to requests for funds or personnel which would enable the agency to forestall such complaints in the future. The generalized complaint regarding county health inspections explicitly criticized administrative performance, and implicitly suggested a possible need for legislative action to establish more stringent requirements. The "combined" complaint involving payment of non-resident tuition fees directly questioned the equity of state policy incorporated in the education code. (We might note, parenthetically, that the legislator's response to the County Health Department complaint indicates a capacity to overlook political boundaries which might considerably enhance his effectiveness in dealing with misdirected or inter-jurisdictional complaints.)

Judging from data on the agencies most frequently contacted, there appears to be little qualitative difference in the bulk of complaint mail received in the offices of the Governor and state legislators: far and away the most prominent targets of complaint are the Departments of Social Welfare, Employment, and Motor Vehicles. The extent to which complaints tend to cluster in these areas would seem to facilitate the development of expertise and of regular channels of communication for dealing with the target agencies. However, ability to take advantage of the opportunity is conditioned by (1) the number of complaints received (too few will not permit conventionalized responses, too many will require superficial responses), and (2) rapidity of turnover in the Legislature itself, and in the offices of the Governor and individual legislators.

While our three data sources are in essential agreement as to the agencies most frequently complained about, there are some discrepancies regarding the people who most frequently complain. In Professor Mann's sample of the summer complaint mail received by three legislators, 66 of 81 cases are attributed to "middle-class people," and only 15 to "the impoverished, the ignorant, or the desperate." In a self-selected sample including 16 of 40 Democratic administrative assistants, "middle class" people were rated the most frequent source of complaints, but they were followed closely by "poorer people," and somewhat further by "minority groups." (Declining to play the rating game when asked to describe the kinds of people who contacted his office, one A.A. replied, "All classes—the rich want favors, the poor want help. The middle class wants identity and the 'cranks' want more representation.")

There is no comparable data on the origin of complaints to the Governor's office, but referrals to the Departments of Social Welfare and Employment nearly equal those to a total of 31 other administrative agencies, indicating that a substantial number of complaints originate outside the middle class. Professor McDaniel has remarked elsewhere that "if there is a group that complains often, it is made up of a high percentage of the sick, the elderly, and racial minorities." Despite obvious problems of extrapolation and definition, the differences are suggestive. It might be inferred that (1) there are substantial variations among legislative districts with respect to the primary sources of complaint mail; (2) based upon comparisons among Professor Mann's sample, the more extensive sample of administrative assistants, and the observation of legislators representing urban districts, these variations are partly traceable to the socio-economic characteristics of the district, and (3) there are significant differences in the sources of complaint mail to the Governor and state legislators, possibly attributable to the Governor's greater visibility to "the impoverished, the ignorant, or the desperate."

Closely related to the above are differences in the volume of complaint mail received. The sample of administrative assistants indicated a mean of eighteen complaints per week, but the range extended from one to fifty. Two of the legislators included in Professor Mann's study averaged fewer than four complaints a week, while Assembly Speaker Unruh is reported to get 100, and a state Senator from south Los Angeles receives so many complaints that—according to his administrative assistant—his office hasn't a prayer of looking at them all, let alone doing something about them. Judging from this very sketchy data, the volume of complaint mail received would appear to be in part a function of the socio-economic composition of the district, and in part a function of the perceived influence or other distinguishing characteristics of the recipient. (The Senator is the only Negro member of the California Senate, and he receives complaints from people located throughout the state.)

It would be tempting to make some comparisons between the gross volume of complaint mail received by the Governor and the legislature, looking for indications that a remote but highly visible Governor attracts more complaints than a less remote but also less visible state legislator. We have scarcely been circumspect about venturing onto thin data, but a line must be drawn somewhere. We will therefore restrict our hypothesis to the legislator's role. It runs as follows: the effectiveness of state legislators in handling citizen complaints will vary directly with the simplicity, repetitiveness, and general policy implications of the complaints received, and inversely with their volume.

STAFF ASSISTANCE FOR COMPLAINT-HANDLING

We have discussed the important roles played by the legislator's assistants and the Governor's staff secretaries in connection with attitudes toward complaint-handling. Here we will concentrate on the activities and potential of the professional staff of legislative committees.

Within the limits of their jurisdiction and the capacity of their staff, legislative committees offer a promising avenue for reducing the legislator's dependence upon the administrative agencies complained about, while at the same time relieving pressure on his personal staff. Since the committee's work is specialized, its staff can develop a measure of expertise beyond the reach of individual offices; since the responsibilities of standing committees are continuing, they can provide a stability of tenure which few legislators can match, and since the committees serve as central reference points, they are in a position to recognize patterns of complaint which would be imperceptible to individual legislators.

Although the committees of Congress enjoy similar advantages, their potential for providing assistance in handling complaints has not been exploited. According to Kenneth Kofmehl, "Except for the 'service' or 'watchdog' committee staffs, case work did not constitute a major fraction of their overall workloads, ten to fifteen per cent being the average estimate of the committee aides interviewed." [6] Have state legislators been any more alert to the complaint-handling potential of their professionally staffed committees? Once again we confront a data gap, but thanks to the cooperation of three interns attached to committees of California's lower house—Bruce Robeck, Assembly Committee on Education; Trent Feldman, Assembly Committee on Public Health; and Richard Buck, Assembly Committee on Revenue and Taxation—some fragmentary information is available.

Despite the relevance of their jurisdictions to programs which often occasion complaints, the most striking observation about the experience of these committees is the infrequency with which they are asked to deal with citizen complaints. Excluding instant responses to oral inquiries and bills "which may be classified as the culmination of a problem of administrative discretion," the Education committee handled an average of two to three "hard-core" cases per month; Public Health an average of four per month during the period preceding the regular session, and ten per month thereafter; and, Revenue and Taxation an average of three per month during the session. Of the trickle of complaints referred to the committees' staff, the vast majority involved administrative or statutory policies, mainly relating to application, filing and eligibility requirements. (A good example of the complaints referred to these committees can be seen in the non-resident tuition fee case cited above.) The only substantial exception involved complaints to the Public Health committee from relatives of state mental hospital patients.

The sources of complaints referred to the three committees varied

[6] Kenneth Kofmehl, *Professional Staffs of Congress* (Purdue University Studies: West Lafayette, Indiana, 1962), p. 128. See also Dale Vinyard, "Congressional Committees on Small Business," *Midwest Journal of Political Science, 10,* No. 3 (August 1966), 364-77.

somewhat, but the sample is too small to permit useful inferences: the Education committee received the majority of its complaints through referrals from members' offices; complaints received by the Public Health committee were typically sent directly to the chairman; and, the Revenue and Taxation committee received complaints in almost equal number by referral and directly from the complainant. In each instance a few of the direct complaints involved a constituent of the chairman. These were given priority, but their number was insignificant.

Here is one intern's unvarnished summary of the procedures followed in responding to complaints referred to his committee. While this account may not be representative, it nicely illustrates the committee's potential for reinforcing the complaint-handling capability of individual legislators:

1. Get more detail on the complaint if the information is sketchy or incomplete.
2. Verify the accuracy of the complaint:
   a. consult statutory law if applicable.
   b. discuss the problem with other staff members if you are not familiar with the particular area.
3. Call the head of the agency, division, or bureau that handles the problem (never, never waste time with a secretary—legislative staff has *very* free access to high ranking administrative officials). If you know someone in lower administrative levels—but not too low—service may be speeded.
4. Note official answer, but maintain independent evaluation of both complaint and answer. The answer to the persons who make the complaint may be a repetition of the official line or it may contain information or facts not available to the complaining party. Follow up on individual cases is not too frequent.

While the process as a whole reflects a more expert and objective evaluation than could be obtained in the offices of most legislators, the final comment suggests that the committee staff has a rather narrow view of its obligations in handling complaints. This inference is substantiated by a number of specific examples: although hardly overburdened by voluminous complaints, the committees have often failed to take advantage of their opportunity to explore the broader implications of a particular case or pattern of cases.

We would hypothesize that where legislative committees are equipped with a competent professional staff, the extent to which it is used for complaint-handling will depend upon (1) the attitudes of the chairman and his chief of staff, including partisan bias as well as internal priorities; (2) discriminations made by individual legislators between policy and administrative complaints; (3) the tenure of all concerned—assuming the stability of the committee staff, novice legislators and their assistants may be more inclined to look to the committee for help. On the other hand, particular committee aides may develop reputations for expertise and cooperativeness which will be better known to seasoned legislators and their personal staff.

Results: Real and Perceived

What happens when a state legislator or staff secretary to the Governor intercedes on the complainant's behalf? On the basis of data contained in the studies we have cited so extensively, one is tempted to reply, "very little"—but this response would rest on a narrow interpretation of specific outcomes, and it would largely ignore the perceptions of the participants.

THE COMPLAINANT

Since we have no data directly measuring the opinions of those who complain, our ranking must be conjectural. In order of their *likely* value to the complainant, the tangible results of intercessions in his behalf include: (1) a specific decision reversed or revised to the complainant's advantage; (2) a general policy softened or shelved; (3) a private bill enacted exempting a narrowly-defined class of complainants; (4) the provision of fuller information which approximates a different result through its specification of options or false assumptions; (5) more sympathetic consideration by agency officials (although the influence implicity attributed to the intervenor can seldom be verified); (6) improved channels of communication with appropriate authorities; (7) expedited treatment of pending actions; (8) policy re-evaluation; (9) improved understanding of state policy where the basis of the complaint proves to be factually incorrect; (10) independent confirmation of the administrative agency's prior response.

Judging from the estimates of Democratic administrative assistants, the results most commonly obtained run in nearly reverse order of their value to the complainant. Our case materials yield at least one example of every alternative but the first. Specific decisions may be reversed on occasion, but this is universally rated the least probable outcome. The administrative assistants ranked the most important functions performed for the citizen as follows: (1) providing a sense of being represented in government; (2) speeding up consideration of the complaint or problem; (3) obtaining more sympathetic consideration through advocacy; (4) helping citizens to understand state policy, and (5) obtaining state agency decisions different from what would have been obtained without the legislator's intervention. It is noteworthy that the most highly rated function involves an assumed perception, rather than a tangible result. (The assumption itself, however, is supported by frequent expressions of gratitude from complainants.)

With the exception of prison inmates—and possibly members of minority groups—aggrieved citizens who appeal to the Governor are even less likely to get tangible results. "Routine" complaints and problems falling outside the Governor's jurisdiction are siphoned off by the Correspondence Unit, which is geared for rapid disposition of voluminous mail. It will probably refer the complaint to the target agency for a direct response, or reply by form letter. The bulk of the remaining correspondence is directed to the Assistant Cabinet Secretary, whose limited ability to provide individual treatment is suggested by McDaniel's analysis of mail processed during May of 1964. Exclusive of autotyped letters and file copies, a total of 1,453 pieces of mail were handled: nearly 80 per cent were either answered by form letter (620) or referred to the target agency for a direct reply (524); 152 were answered by dictated letters, 51 were referred to target agencies for suggested replies, and 106 were answered on the basis of the agencies' suggested replies. Complaint mail probably accounted for no more than one-third of the total, but even if we assume that most of the form letters and agency referrals did not involve complaints, there seems to be little prospect of getting a more satisfactory result by writing the Governor than by dealing directly with the agency. Since every letter receives *some* reply, that elusive "sense of being represented in government" may be served again—but there is no evidence comparable to that cited by state legislators.

Once the constituent's complaint percolates down to the administrator who oversees a highly decentralized organization, the likelihood of thorough consideration is only slightly improved, as Professor McDaniel's analysis of California's Resources Agency indicates:

> . . . first, there is no method of checking the mail that goes directly to the departments; and second, there is no way to determine the degree to which an answer has satisfied a citizen who does not respond to the answer itself. An agency spokesman expressed the belief that a correspondent must continue to persevere if the agency is to become fully aware that his complaint is legitimate.

THE LEGISLATOR

In the absence of data systematically tracing the origin of legislation to constituent complaints, demonstrating that citizen alienation has been reduced through complaint work, or indicating that campaign assistance was volunteered as a result of efforts to help complainants, all payoffs to legislators must be regarded as perceived. As our caveat suggests, the advantages which are believed to accrue to the legislator fall into three broad categories, relating to (1) his legislative activity oriented toward state-wide policies, (2) his representation of immediate constituent interests, and (3) his reelection or candidacy for higher office. In the first category would be the role played by complaints in alerting the legislator to administrative problems or statutory inequities which might call for corrective legislation; in the second, the opportunity they provide to forge a link between the citizen and his increasingly complex government. As to the assumed political benefits of complaint work, they are neatly captured in the phrases of our administrative assistants: "Good will. Word of mouth publicity. Volunteer assistance during the campaign;" "Most constituents don't forget at election time that they have been helped by your member's office;" "Community leaders feel he's on the ball;" "He gets reelected or steps up the political ladder because he serves the people."

Apart from their intangibility, the most striking feature of all the preceding benefits is their dependence upon the legislator's ability to do a decent job of servicing his constituent's complaints. If he receives only three or four complaints a week, he may have time to consider their policy implications, or to seek a resolution that will inspire the constituent to contribute money and services in his next campaign. Indeed, an Assemblyman in Professor Mann's sample who represents a marginal district and receives a modest volume of complaint mail actually solicits complaints. At the other extreme, the state Senator from south Los Angeles is the recipient of so many complaints that concern with the policy implications of individual grievances is out of sight; citizen alienation is if anything increased by his inability to give complaints the attention he feels they deserve, and the cost of unanswered complaints counterbalances the political benefits accruing from those pursued. It is noteworthy that both of these legislators have actively supported California's Ombudsman proposal. Although impressed with its potential for serving his constituents' needs, the Senator sees no realistic alternative simply in terms of his own self-interest. While the Assemblyman has a greater incentive and opportunity to capitalize on constituent service, he does not view Ombudsman as threatening to his roles as either politician or legislator.

THE GOVERNOR

Payoffs to the Governor will be disposed of quickly—although they may be considerable, they are exceedingly remote. It was the impression of his staff that the Governor took a personal interest in answering citizen complaints, and most of them shared this interest. Their priorities are indicative of the value they placed on complaint work: "First, they want to answer correspondents, and to give them as much satisfaction as possible. In addition, they are strongly motivated to enhance the Governor's public image. In this respect, there is an element of public relations in the answering and handling of citizen complaints."

THE ADMINISTRATIVE AGENCY

Whether viewed from the perspective of the complainant or the target agency, the tangible results of informal complaint-handling will be the same. Although a few categories are not equally appropriate, our classification of benefits accruing to individual and agency are virtual mirror images of one another—with some of the parts and most of the weights reversed. They include: (1) independent confirmation to the complainant that the agency's original action was correct; (2) improved understanding of agency policy and procedures resulting from fuller—and again, independent—explanations; (3) more effective communication with members of the agency's clientele, especially those who are reluctant to complain to the agency for fear of losing existing benefits, those who are ignorant of filing requirements, and those who do not know which agency to contact; (4) more sympathetic consideration of agency problems by the Governor and members of the Legislature—these would include budget, statutory mandate, and the burden of chronic complainers; (5) provision of additional data permitting a better-informed decision; (6) indications of need for policy revision or procedural reform, and (7) evidence of extenuating circumstances permitting an exception in the particular case. Presumably this would not become important until the agency perceived a high degree of political interest in the outcome, and required some basis for justifying an extraordinary decision.

Our hypothesis is that the results most frequently obtained through informal complaint-handling run in direct order of their probable value to the target agencies, and reverse order of their probable value to the complainant. This suggests that the Governor's office and the Legislature are generally providing services which are more advantageous to the agency than to the complainant. If the indicated conclusion should prove to be correct, it would offer a significant commentary on the efficacy of informal machinery for handling citizen complaints.

Conclusion

We began this essay with a list of objectives and attributes associated with Ombudsman. In the interim we have been concerned with the collection and analysis of data required to test the validity of assumptions regarding the capacity of more conventional instruments of state government to do the same job. What conclusions are suggested by this analysis?

FORMAL INSTRUMENTALITIES

Within its jurisdiction, and given increased accessibility, California's Commission on Judicial Qualifications affords a viable alternative to Ombudsman. Of the other instrumentalities examined, (1) the performance of independent offices and legislative committees charged with oversight of administrative procedures is not directly relevant in that their work is needed whether or not one has an Ombudsman; (2) joint interim committees and legislative bureaus concerned with administrative organization and efficiency lack sufficient time to consider individual grievances, and sufficient staff to pursue them effectively. If these obstacles could be overcome—and the Wisconsin experience at least raises the possibility that they might be—its committees and bureaus would still appear to be too closely linked with the legislature to be regarded by administrative agencies as objective channels for the redress of citizen grievances.

INFORMAL COMPLAINT-HANDLING MECHANISMS

Based upon limited data concerning the complaint-handling activities of members of the Legislature and of the Governor's staff in California, our general conclusion is that their primary function is to improve the flow of information between agency and complainant. Alternative courses of action may be indicated, the pain of an administrative decision may be eased as a result of independent confirmation or explanation, but seldom is the particular problem resolved to the complainant's satisfaction. Reviewing the desireable consequences earlier attributed to Ombudsman, our evaluation begins on an inauspicious note:

1. The redress of individual grievances is the central objective of an Ombudsman. Present machinery seems to be inadequate to that end.

2. The Ombudsman is also meant to provide protection against improper and inefficient administration through centralized and continuous oversight. No effective instruments for improving administration are discernible in the data which we have examined.

3. To the extent that public confidence in administration depends upon its responsiveness to individual complaints, either the Governor or the Legislature would appear to offer a more direct and comfortable means of keeping administration responsive. But contributions to public confidence in administration ultimately depend upon ability to obtain results which are valued by the citizen, and the effectiveness of both the Governor and state legislators is critically impaired by their dependence on the agencies complained about. An Ombudsman would not suffer this defect.

4. While the performance of legislative functions could hardly be

improved without some change in existing procedures or personnel, it should not be assumed that all state legislators are overburdened with complaints. But where the volume is sufficient to require some trade-off between servicing complaints and attending to legislation, neither should it be assumed that alternatives to Ombudsman would automatically provide equivalent relief. Supervision of an expanded personal staff, for example, would intrude upon time which could be devoted to legislation, where referrals to Ombudsman would not. As to the role played by complaints in flagging general problems of policy or administration, the legislator's perspective is too narrow to permit identification of recurring problems, and his time often insufficient to pursue the broader implications of individual complaints. An Ombudsman could help remedy this shortsightedness.

5. The administrative agencies appear to be the principal beneficiaries of complaint-handling by the Governor's office and the Legislature, but there is no evidence that their contribution is perceived by the agencies, that it is valued, or that it improves morale.

Though informal complaint-handling machinery presently falls short of the goals we have stipulated, what of its potential? If overburdened legislators had additional office help and were able to make more extensive use of capably staffed committees, their dependence on the administrative agencies might be substantially reduced. With sufficient manpower and time, substantive committees might be able to identify patterns of maladministration, and explore the policy implications of specific complaints. If not required to buy time from countless other responsibilities, a complaint specialist in the Governor's office might be able to identify problem agencies or policies, personally explore certain of the more serious complaints, and systematically audit agency responses. Corresponding functions might also be performed by specialists located in the principal administrative departments—Michigan's Secretary of State, for example, has appointed a departmental "Ombudsman."

These are promising options, and they might enable conventional instrumentalities to move a long way toward meeting the objectives sought through Ombudsman. But they fail in their ability to duplicate the essential attributes of Ombudsman:

1. His accessibility. The legislator's potential as a complaint-handler may not be recognized by those most seriously in need of assistance, and where it is recognized, he may not appear accessible to all of his constituents (e.g., an active supporter of his opponent in the preceding election).

2. His impartiality. Legislators and legislative committees are open to suspicion of partisan bias and legislative chauvinism, the Governor's staff of a protective attitude toward administrative agencies.

3. His expertise. Neither the individual offices of state legislators nor the Governor's staff have an opportunity to develop it in proportion to the volume of complaints with which they are confronted, and if they were to fully realize their potential in this regard, legislative committees would be forced to neglect their primary responsibility for policy formulation.

4. His ability to assure uniform treatment. Even if their present inability to determine the capriciousness of agency responses should be reduced, both the Governor and state legislators may be suspected of giving preference to friends and major campaign contributors.

In comparing Ombudsman with the potential of those mechanisms upon which we have traditionally relied for the redress of citizens grievances, it should be emphasized that they are not mutually exclusive alternatives. While Ombudsman might do many things that elected representatives have failed to accomplish—and may be incapable of accomplishing—political officials possess certain advantages. From a practical standpoint, they may have an ability to bridge political boundaries through informal connections which Ombudsman would not share. More significant is the vicarious sense of participation in government which accompanies demands made of elected officials, and the confidence which attaches to concern based upon the politician's self-interest, rather than sterile concepts of legal authority or sound administrative practice.

From an academic point of view, we have clearly established that a great deal more research is needed. Perhaps this research will confirm our tentative conclusions that (1) the performance of existing state mechanisms for handling citizen complaints is inadequate; (2) although their potential may be great, they are incapable of fulfilling the goals we have stipulated for an Ombudsman; and (3) the operation of an Ombudsman will not diminish the value of conventional channels of grievance redress; on the contrary, it will enhance them.

Additional data would also contribute substantially to our knowledge of existing institutions. But so far as Ombudsman is concerned, perhaps the most useful source of data would be the office itself. If performance affords the best means of testing assumptions, we have a relatively low-cost alternative to speculation about Ombudsman at the state level: establish one, and see how it works.

William H. Angus and Milton Kaplan

4

The Ombudsman and
Local Government

We live in an age of government. An increasingly complex society has turned more and more to legislators for solutions to problems beyond the capacity of the private sector. Given this situation, society can ill afford public mistrust of its governmental machinery. Yet suspicion of bureaucracy and maladministration in government is substantial, as indicated in Chapter 2. Procedures for resolution of complaints against public administration are, therefore, of fundamental concern.

Many of these problems are most acute at the local level. Shifting population patterns and urban decay have brought scores of municipal administrations to the brink of economic and social disaster. Recent outbreaks of violence in a number of our heavily populated cities reflect the critical condition of many urban communities. Although Federal and state government policies are unquestionably important

WILLIAM H. ANGUS *is Professor of Law at the State University of New York at Buffalo. A former member of the Faculty of Law at the University of Alberta, he has written a number of articles dealing with the problems of judicial selection, and is author of a Canadian case book on Administrative Law.*

MILTON KAPLAN *is Professor of Law at the State University of New York at Buffalo. Formerly a lawyer in New York City, he has written articles on public law topics, served as First Assistant to the Counsel to the Governor of the State of New York, and was Corporation Counsel to the City of Cortland. He has also served as a planning law consultant to various agencies in New York State and abroad.*

to the individual citizen, he is more directly affected by local government administration. Here the everyday public services like garbage collection, road maintenance, street lighting, traffic control, welfare administration, police security, fire fighting, planning and zoning, public utilities, public transportation and a host of other mundane but essential community functions, strike home to everyone.

People do not readily distinguish between levels of government. Attitudes toward public administration are general in nature, and shaped by personal contact. They are not significantly influenced by Federal, state and local distinctions. Since a citizen's dealings with local government are closer and more frequent, public administration on the local level becomes of critical importance. Hence American adaptation of the Scandinavian Ombudsman institution for resolving complaints of citizens against local government authorities merits serious consideration.

Experience Abroad

With one exception, Ombudsman surveillance of local governmental activities in Scandinavia is of recent origin. Finland's Ombudsman has traditionally concerned himself with administration at all levels of government.[1] The Finnish experience does not suggest any unusual problems attributable to their Ombudsman's local government jurisdiction.

The jurisdiction of the Swedish Ombudsman over local government actions dates back to a constitutional amendment in 1957, though here too his operations at the municipal level are subject to restrictions. Investigation of elected local councils and councilors is specifically excepted. Nor can he intervene until procedures for appeal have been exhausted and the local legislature has failed to act, unless personal liberty is endangered or an obvious abuse of power is evident. Notwithstanding these limitations, the Swedish Ombudsman's role in review of local government activities is both substantial and increasing.[2]

Only since 1962 has the Danish Ombudsman had jurisdiction over local officials, and even then his local jurisdiction is confined to matters with respect to which an appeal lies to central government

[1] Os, "The Ombudsman for Civil Affairs," in Donald C. Rowat, ed., *The Ombudsman* (1965), p. 100.

[2] Bexelius, "The Ombudsman for Civil Affairs," in Donald C. Rowat, ed., *The Ombudsman* (1965), p. 28; Jagerskiold, "The Swedish Ombudsman," 109 *University of Pennsylvania Law Review* (1961), pp. 1082-3; Walter Gellhorn, *Ombudsmen and Others* (1966), p. 208.

authority.[3] Professor Walter Gellhorn in *Ombudsmen and Others* has observed that in "terms of political tact, he appears to proceed very gingerly when dealing with local affairs."

In Norway, the Ombudsman can deal with those municipal administrative matters which are concerned with the deprivation of personal liberty. He may also consider the action of a local administration when the matter reaches a higher level which is within his jurisdiction. Beyond this, the Norwegian Ombudsman cannot delve into local government affairs. A substantial number of complaints addressed to him in 1963 and 1964 were declined because they dealt with municipal matters beyond his jurisdiction. Consideration is now being given to widening the scope of his review over the municipal level.[4]

Local authorities are not within reach of the New Zealand Ombudsman, although some sentiment is developing for putting him in the picture.[5] The arguments for and against that suggestion are similar to those being aired in the cities of the United States—local councilors are (or are not) effectively dealing with citizens' grievances; local autonomy would (or would not) be diminished; the Ombudsman could (or could not) handle the volume of complaints that would be engendered at the local level; the caliber of municipal servants evidences (or does not evidence) the greater need for Ombudsman intervention in the lower reaches of government.

Local Government Ombudsman Proposals in the United States

PHILADELPHIA

In 1962, a "watchdog" committee established by Mayor Richardson Dilworth of Philadelphia and headed by Dean Jefferson B. Fordham of the University of Pennsylvania Law School, recommended the appointment of a Commissioner of Public Affairs for that city with powers similar to those exercised by the Danish Ombudsman. The Committee proposed that the appointment be made by the City

[3] Pedersen, "Denmark's Ombudsmand," in Donald C. Rowat, ed., *The Ombudsman* (1965), pp. 80-1; Christensen, "The Danish Ombudsman," 109 *University of Pennsylvania Law Review* (1961), pp. 1107-8; Hurwitz, "The Danish Parliamentary Commissioner for Civil and Miliary Administration," 1 *Journal of the International Commission of Jurists* (1958), pp. 232-3.

[4] Wold, "The Norwegian Parliament's Commissioner for the Civil Administration," 2 *Journal of the International Commission of Jurists* (No. 2, 1960), p. 26; Os, "The Ombudsman for Civil Affairs," in Donald C. Rowat, ed., *The Ombudsman* (1965), pp. 100-1, 323, 325; Walter Gellhorn, *Ombudsmen and Others* (1966), pp. 167-8.

[5] Northey, "New Zealand's Parliamentary Commissioner," in Donald C. Rowat, ed., *The Ombudsman* (1965), p. 135; Walter Gellhorn, *Ombudsmen and Others* (1966), pp. 114-8; Powles, "The Ombudsman: The Champion of the Citizen," 21 *The Record of the Association of the Bar of the City of New York* (1966), p. 403.

Council from two or three nominees of a group composed of such outsiders as the president of one of the local universities, the Chancellor of the Philadelphia Bar Association, and the President of the Philadelphia Chamber of Commerce.[6]

Professor Henry J. Abraham of the University of Pennsylvania noted that the proposal "was met with a veritable barrage of frank hostility and intemperate criticism on the part of the segments of the community that comprise the seat of power, led by the three daily newspapers, the incumbent political leadership in City Council, and the Democratic City Committee;" that the press saw in the proposal "an unwarranted expense and just another 'politician on top of a bunch of politicians'," and as an " 'ivory tower lark';" while the City Council "saw it as an 'unnecessary' and unknown quantity of conceivably awkward if not 'dangerous' potential." [7]

Needless to add, the proposal was killed in a Council Committee. But it did spur the Mayor to establish by executive decree a "Director of Citizens' Relations," characterized by Professor Abraham as "more of a complaint bureau and . . . more of a peripatetic trouble-shooter and general 'sniffer' than a tribune of the people."

NEW YORK CITY

Perhaps uniquely, the history of efforts to establish an Ombudsman for New York City includes episodes in the development of parallel institutions for redressing governmental excesses.

In 1961, Mayor Robert F. Wagner provided a special mailing address—"Box 100, New York, N.Y."—for complaints of official misconduct. Then in 1963, the Mayor turned over the key to his Department of Investigation. Since 1873 when that office was created as a Commissioner of Accounts to deal with manipulations of the Tweed Ring, the department had been regarded primarily as the Mayor's investigator of corruption by public officials. The Department of Investigation was charged by law in the 1963 transfer of power, however, to "receive complaints from the public." Box 100 seemed to have transformed the department into a full-fledged instrument for dealing with public grievances, bearing a strong resemblance to the foreign Ombudsman.

In November, 1966, the Commissioner of Investigation reported that since the beginning of that year, the department had handled 4,819 complaints, more than 3,000 of them originating from Box 100 mail. Six months later, at a panel discussion sponsored by the Associa-

---

[6] *Report of the Mayor's Ad Hoc Committee on Improvement in Municipal Standards and Practices,* quoted in part in the *Local Government Service Letter* of the Section of Local Government, American Bar Association (1966).

[7] Henry J. Abraham, "The Need for Ombudsmen in the United States," in Donald C. Rowat, ed., *The Ombudsman* (1965), pp. 238-39.

tion of the Bar of the City of New York, the Commissioner reported that complaints were being registered with his office at a rate of about 30 per day and predicted that about 9,000 complaints would be processed during the fiscal year 1966-67. A major portion of the department's annual budget of $1 million and about 90 percent of its activities are now devoted to investigating alleged oversight, arrogance and other frailties of city functionaries far less serious than the venality traditionally pursued by the Commissioner of Investigation. The Commissioner has provided a personal touch to the processing of public complaints, characteristic of the Ombudsman, in his practice of signing individually typed letters to officials against whom complaints are registered. As shall be noted later, these developments in the Department of Investigation have been used to question the establishment of a separate Ombudsman office for New York City.

In contrast, events of the same period relating to the New York City Police Department's Civilian Complaint Review Board have given support to a counterthrust toward the creation of an Ombudsman. When the review board in 1965 consisted of three Deputy Police Commissioners, two of them lawyers and one a former police reporter, civil rights leaders promoted the substitution of an independent civilian review panel operating outside of the police department. Congressman John V. Lindsay, as candidate for mayor, proposed instead the addition of four civilian members to the existing police department board. The then Police Commissioner, Vincent L. Broderick, and the Patrolmen's Benevolent Association adamantly opposed both moves.

The issue did not die with the implementation of the Lindsay plan after he became mayor. Instead it was put to the city electorate on November 8, 1966 in the form of a referendum on a proposition barring the use of outsiders on the police department's review board. This issue was the hottest contest on the ballot that election day. Those favoring the use of outside members as a "safety valve for the release of minority grievances" warned that their elimination would bring riots in the ghettos of New York City. Opponents contended that the continued use of civilian outsiders would undermine the administrative authority of the Police Commissioner, and destroy the morale and efficiency of the police department. The proposition carried by an overwhelming vote of 1,307,738 to 768,492. A resulting prohibition against packing the board with outsiders gave fresh impetus to the movement to create a separate office of Ombudsman.

Seeking to make good on another campaign pledge, Mayor Lindsay in 1966 established three Neighborhood City Halls to provide information and referral services, but the Board of Estimate and City Council refused to provide special budgetary support. In January,

1967, the Mayor asked the City Council to pass a local law setting up 27 Neighborhood City Halls, each to serve a Council district. Perhaps to counter opposition charges that Neighborhood City Halls would become "Lindsay political club houses," the proposed law would have given each Council member a veto power over the selection of one-half the staff of his district's office. When the Mayor expressed himself in favor of the Ombudsman concept and pointed to Ombudsman elements in his Neighborhood City Halls plan, the opposition argued that establishment of a general office for receiving public complaints would be preferable.

Neighborhood City Halls—or "Little City Halls" as they are popularly known—were subsequently established by executive order. They have proved to be strong magnets for public complaints. The director of the Bronx unit counted 1,356 written grievances processed by his office between December 1, 1966 and the middle of May, 1967. These have been handled by a staff of regular city employees aided by volunteers, despite the lack of a separate budget.

While the foregoing scenes were being acted out, willing Ombudsmen were standing in the wings. In 1965 and 1966, bills were introduced in the City Council to create an "Office of Citizen Redress," and in the latter year an alternative proposal placed before the Council called for creation of an office of "Administrative Review" as an arm of the Council. On May 11, 1967, the City Council President, Frank D. O'Connor—who had sponsored one of the measures for establishing an Office of Citizen Redress—filed a new version which had been prepared by the Committee on Administrative Law of the Association of the Bar of the City of New York. It has been supported by an impressive block of civil leaders and officials, including the former Police Commissioner, Vincent L. Broderick, who had broken with the Mayor over the issue of the composition of the Police Department's Civilian Complaint Review Board.

The Bar Committee's proposal would create an Office of Public Complaint, headed by an "Ombudsman".[8] This Ombudsman would be appointed by the Mayor with the advice and consent of the City Council. The bill's statement of policy calls for appointment of "a person of distinguished accomplishments in the field of law or administration," and specifies as the "main functions" of the office:

> (a) to investigate and ameliorate grievances arising out of allegations of agency maladministration, unfairness, unreasonableness, arbitrariness, arrogance, rudeness, oppressiveness, inefficiency, improper motivation, unwarranted delay, clear violations of laws or regulations, or other abuse of

[8] "Proposed Local Law for a New York City Ombudsman," Report of the Committee on Administrative Law, in 22 *The Record of The Association of the Bar of the City of New York* (1967), p. 486.

authority, and (b) on its own initiative, to investigate, study and make recommendations with regard to agency acts, practices and procedures.

Jurisdiction of the Ombudsman would extend to any department or other governmental unit, "other than (1) the board of estimate only insofar as it acts as a board, (2) the council, its members and their staffs, (3) the courts, and (4) the mayor, the deputy mayors, their assistants and their staffs."

Concern was expressed by the Bar's Committee on Administrative Law with the need to "insulate the Ombudsman from politics as much as possible." The Committee thought this would be achieved by providing for his appointment by both the Mayor and the Council, and by giving him a term of five years which would overlap that of the Mayor. Various other devices were discarded, such as the use of a nominating panel composed of reputable citizens, as being unworkable. The bill also provides for the repeal of the City Charter provisions empowering the Department of Investigation to receive complaints from the public. Activities of that complaint bureau, and corresponding budgetary appropriations, would be transferred to the new Office of Public Complaint. The Commissioner of Investigation would continue to exercise his function of making investigations as directed by the Mayor or City Council.

As of June, 1967, the Mayor seems to have favored a move in the opposite direction. In the panel discussion sponsored by the Association of the Bar of the City of New York held on June 20, 1967, his Commissioner of Investigation intimated that the Mayor would propose modifications subjecting the appointment of the Commissioner of Investigation to approval of the City Council, and changing the term of the Commissioner's office from an indefinite one, at the pleasure of the Mayor, to a fixed five-year period. Possibly looking to the absorption of the complaint handling function of the Neighborhood City Halls, the Commissioner stated that the Mayor was also contemplating establishment by the Department of Investigation of neighborhood field offices whose staffs would receive complaints, and where possible, process them on the spot.

If the method of appointment, term of office and functions of the Commissioner of Investigation would be similar to those of the proposed Ombudsman, why then should New York City opt for a new office? According to proponents of the Ombudsman bill, the answer lies in the fact that to be effective the Ombudsman must be completely independent of the executive establishment, and the Commissioner of Investigation, so long identified with the Mayor of the city, does not meet that test. Critics of the Mayor's proposal concede that the Mayor should have his own investigative arm for his own purposes, but this should be a parallel instrumentality of government and not a substitute for the independent office of Ombudsman—just as the Chancellor of Justice in Sweden exists side by side with the *Justitieombudsman.*

NEW YORK STATE: PROPOSED LEGISLATION

In the years 1965 to 1967, a number of bills were introduced in the New York Legislature to authorize the establishment of a state-level Ombudsman. Among these, the Dunne-Jonas bill (A. 4013/1967; S. 2684/1967) proposed appointment by the State Legislature of an Ombudsman whose jurisdiction would extend to every

> . . . department, division, bureau, board, commission, authority, office or other unit of government of the state and any political subdivision thereof, [except] the judiciary, any legislative body, the governor, lieutenant governor, attorney general or comptroller of the state, the district attorney of any county and any chief executive or legislative body of any political subdivision thereof.

In their memorandum supporting the bill, Senator John R. Dunne and Assemblyman Milton Jonas asserted that by bringing all levels of government within the jurisdiction of the State Ombudsman, the "public will initially be spared inevitable proliferation of the office that would otherwise result," and the "confusion and frustration" of having to choose between "multiple ombudsmen." Yet the bill does not prohibit the establishment of municipal Ombudsmen and at least one of the provisions would appear to accommodate competing local-level Ombudsmen—the provision authorizing the State Ombudsman to refuse to investigate any complaint which is "already under investigation by another office . . ."

New York State has 3,405 separate, independent units of local government—cities, counties, towns, villages, school districts, fire districts—aside from improvement districts and other local authorities. The Dunne-Jonas proposal poses a dilemma. A state Ombudsman could hardly give personal attention to more than a small fraction of the complaints involving so sizeable and varied a collection of municipal entities. To the bulk of such complainants, he would be regarded as a high and distant appellate authority concerned only with the rare dispute that cannot be settled locally and quickly, and serious enough to the complainant to justify processing upwards through a hierarchy of officers in the Ombudsman's establishment. Or he might be regarded as another version of the State Commission of Investigation, concerned only with the most serious forms of local corruption, and in such cases perhaps an inadequate substitute for that Commission.

Would the average citizen with a local problem look to a local deputy or employee of a state Ombudsman for ultimate relief? Maybe not. And would the degree of cooperation accorded by a local official depend on his assessment of the skill, integrity and muscle of the particular deputy or employee Ombudsman assigned to his area? We think so. Accordingly, the Dunne-Jonas mechanism for dealing with complaints against local officials might turn out to be an "Ombudsman" in name only. Had their version of a state Ombudsman been operating in the Bronx between December, 1966, and the middle of May, 1967, in lieu of Mayor Lindsay's program, the 1,356 persons who registered complaints during that period at a Little City Hall would have dealt instead with a complaint officer in a "Little State Capitol"— not with an Ombudsman cast from the Scandinavian mold.

WASHINGTON, D.C.

On August 30, 1966, Senator Edward V. Long of Missouri, Chairman of the Senate Subcommittee on Administrative Practice and Procedure, introduced a bill in the Senate (S. 3783) to create an Ombudsman for the District of Columbia. The proposed Ombudsman would be appointed by the President with the advice and consent of the Senate, and granted "jurisdiction to investigate the administrative acts of any agency of the District of Columbia" on his own motion, or on any oral or written complaint of any resident of the District. Specifically excluded from his scrutiny were acts of any court, any agency of the Federal Government, "any multistate governmental entity or compact," or of the Commissioners of the District of Columbia and their personal staff.

Senator Long asserted that the office of Ombudsman would be especially suitable for the District of Columbia because, absent "home rule" giving the citizens of the District their own elected representatives, there is no Mayor or Councilman to or through whom a citizen or taxpayer may submit his grievances. The 1966 bill did not leave Committee, but died at the end of the session. It was reintroduced on January 24, 1967, as S. 626, and again referred to the Committee on the District of Columbia.

KANSAS CITY, MISSOURI

Serious efforts to establish a local government Ombudsman have been made in Jackson County, Missouri, which includes Kansas City. Bill No. 511, introduced in the Missouri House of Representatives on February 21, 1967 by Representative Ken Growney, passed the House only to die in the Missouri Senate when its session expired on June 30, 1967. It proposed the establishment of an Ombudsman on the County government level. Its companion Bill No. 486, proposing a State Ombudsman, remained in the House Judiciary Committee.

Perhaps the most interesting feature of both Bills was the insertion of a procedure for choosing an Ombudsman based on the merit selection plan for judges pioneered by the State of Missouri in 1940 and widely known as "The Missouri Plan." Its primary objective is the removal of partisan politics from the selection process. The bills would require appointment of an Ombudsman from a list of three persons nominated by the appropriate non-partisan judicial commission established under the Constitution of Missouri for selection of judges. In the case of a county Ombudsman, the appointment would be made by the appropriate county court from nominations proposed by the non-partisan circuit judicial commission. Another feature of the Missouri Plan known as the retention ballot was included in Bill No. 511. Under this provision, the name of the Ombudsman would be inserted on the judicial ballot at the next county general election following his selection to determine whether the voters wish to retain or reject him.

Insertion of a non-partisan nominating commission and retention ballot is a novel approach to the Ombudsman selection question, and worthy of serious consideration. Its drawback may well be that the Ombudsman has traditionally been a creature of the legislative arm of government. Whether a selection procedure designed for the judiciary would be satisfactory, therefore, is a legitimate issue.

OAKLAND

As in New York City, a campaign to install an Ombudsman in Oakland, California early in 1966 was linked with the prior rejection of civilian review of complaints against the police. But unlike New York City, in Oakland the leader of the campaign for an Ombudsman was the Mayor himself. In February, 1967, the City Council tabled Mayor John H. Reading's request for a special meeting to consider his proposal to set up a "citizen's grievance representative," action that the *Oakland Tribune* on February 8th described in the front-page banner headline:

"Council Slams Door on 'Ombudsman' Proposal."

Council opposition reportedly stemmed from the feeling that the proposal too closely resembled a watered-down version of the civilian police review board which the Council and Mayor had previously rejected, and that it reflected on the way City Hall in general and the police department in particular were handling citizen complaints. The *Oakland Tribune* endorsed the Mayor's objective with a favorable editorial on March 8, 1967, but questioned whether either an appointive or elected Ombudsman would be non-partisan—whether he would be truly independent of the appointing authority if appointed, or afflicted with the normal "overpowering urge to adopt the popular rather than the proper course" in resolving citizen complaints if elected.

Mayor Reading, in taking his case to the public, countered with the revelation that only about 20 per cent of complaints received by the City concerned the police. He stressed the special need to provide an independent grievance officer who would gain the public confidence of Oakland's large "minority groups who feel the cards are stacked against them." [9] On April 18, 1967, Mayor Reading was re-elected with a large majority. Action on the Ombudsman plank in his platform does not yet appear to have developed.

HAWAII

By action concluded in April, 1967, the Hawaiian Legislature was the first legislative body in the United States officially to endorse the Ombudsman idea. Under the Hawaiian Ombudsman Act of 1967, an Ombudsman is to be appointed by a majority vote of each house of the State Legislature in joint session. No appointment could be made by the 1967 Legislature, however, because the measure only became law 45 days after the Legislature had adjourned, without the Governor's signature. According to the *Honolulu Advertiser* of June 14, 1967, the Governor's inaction indicated that he did not approve of the measure, "but is bowing to the intent of the Legislature in passing it "

Though not explicitly, jurisdiction of the Hawaiian Ombudsman does extend to municipal agencies under the Act. It covers the acts of any "permanent governmental entity, department, organization, or institution, and any officer, employee, or member thereof acting or purporting to act in the exercise of his official duties," except a court, the Legislature, the Federal Government, a multistate governmental entity, and the Governor and his personal staff. Report No. 76 dated March 30, 1967 of the Legislature's Standing Committee on Federal-State-County Relations and Government Efficiency, to which the proposal had been referred, declared that the purpose of the office of the Hawaiian Ombudsman was "to protect the citizens of this state against abuses of governmental power by state and county 'agencies'."

Executive Ombudsmen

NASSAU COUNTY

To Nassau County on Long Island in the State of New York goes the distinction of having put into operation the world's first experiment based largely on the Ombudsman principle and designed to

[9] "Citizen Grievance Procedure," speech delivered by Mayor John H. Reading to the American Society for Public Administration, Fairmont Hotel, San Francisco, March 28, 1967.

operate exclusively on the local government level. On May 31, 1966, Nassau County Executive Eugene H. Nickerson issued Executive Order No. 4 empowering his Commissioner of Accounts to assume the powers and duties of Public Protector in accordance with a proposed local law presented on the same day to the Nassau County Board of Supervisors, the County's legislative arm. Contemporaneously, Nickerson appointed Judge Samuel Greason to the vacant Commissioner of Accounts post, pending approval of Public Protector legislation by the Board of Supervisors and a voter referendum.

The Board of Supervisors responded by establishing a special advisory committee chaired by Nassau County District Attorney William Cahn and including as one of its members Joseph L. Marino, counsel to an organization called Operation Task Force. Cahn and Marino visited Scandinavian countries to study the Ombudsman systems in operation there, and England to discuss British proposals for a similar institution.

In his report to the special advisory committee, Cahn opposed an executive role in selection of the Public Protector as proposed by the County Executive, favoring legislative appointment and removal by the Board of Supervisors instead.[10] He also recommended against the County Executive's provision for a six-member advisory council to the Public Protector, and proposed exclusion of the courts and law enforcement agencies from the Public Protector's jurisdiction. In a separate presentation, Marino argued for selection by unanimous approval of the County Executive and Board of Supervisors.[11] All non-elected public servants—including law enforcement agencies but excluding the judiciary—were considered by him to be appropriate for surveillance by the County Ombudsman.

A few months later, the special advisory committee issued its report appending a draft local law providing for a Commissioner of Information and Complaints empowered to investigate actions of appointed County officials but exempting police departments, the judiciary and the District Attorney's office. In August, 1967, the Board of Supervisors proposed a draft local law excepting only the police department from the Public Protector's jurisdiction, a compromise subsequently agreed to by County Executive Nickerson. Approval by the County voters in a referendum will be required before the Public Protector's office achieves final sanction.[12]

---

[10] Cahn, *Ombudsman Report* (Mineola, N.Y., 1966), pp. 4-9, 23-25.

[11] Marino, *A Detailed Study on the Need for the Office of Public Protector (Ombudsman),* (Garden City, N.Y., 1966), pp. 17, 30.

[12] On November 7, 1967, after this manuscript went to press, the proposed Nassau County Public Protector legislation was rejected by the County electors by a vote of 261,902 to 196,260.

In these circumstances, Judge Greason has carried on as Commissioner of Accounts under the County Executive order. In fact, the lack of specific legislation establishing the office of Public Protector has not been viewed as a disadvantage by the incumbent Commissioner of Accounts. As matters now stand, he is relatively free to pursue his work unencumbered by legislative limitations. Most of his accomplishments have been achieved by persuasion and cooperation, the lack of express definition in local law of his powers being of little practical consequence.

The Man for the Office—At this point, a comment on the right person for the position is pertinent. First and perhaps foremost, he must be non-partisan.

Judge Greason was a lifetime Republican, but his independence in thought and action had been firmly established long before his appointment as Commissioner of Accounts by County Executive Nickerson, a Democrat. Speaking for the Republican majority on the Board of Supervisors shortly after Greason's appointment, Ralph G. Casa of Hempstead expressed concern only for "possible abuses by some appointed ominous Ombudsman who might one day succeed the distinguished jurist." Greason accepted the Ombudsman role on Nickerson's assurance that no executive or political interference would hamper the carrying out of his responsibilities. He is quick to assert that the County Executive's undertaking in this regard has been strictly observed.

A lawyer by profession, Judge Greason enjoyed a distinguished record as a judge of the District Court in Nassau County from 1937 to 1958, interrupted only by service in World War II on top of his World War I record. Among other attainments, he had been President of the Nassau County Bar Association in 1948 and 1949, and in 1959 was designated Chief Counsel for the Judicial Inquiry on Professional Conduct by the Appellate Division, Second Judicial Department, of the New York Supreme Court to investigate legal ethics complaints against Long Island lawyers. He resigned from this position to accept the appointment as Commissioner of Accounts. Thus his stature in the community assures an independence free from pressures of any kind.

Staff—Judge Greason endeavors to deal personally with every complaint. Assisting him is his Deputy Commissioner of Accounts. Among other functions, the Deputy Commissioner interviews aggrieved citizens when the Commissioner is otherwise occupied. Investigation of complaints, if required, is carried out chiefly by the Deputy Commissioner and an Assistant Deputy.

Clerical work is performed by two secretaries. An accountant has also been authorized, but to this point Greason has not found it necessary to employ one. Its small size makes the Nassau County Ombudsman's office a highly personalized operation.

Volume of Complaints—In his first year of operation, the Nassau County Ombudsman handled over 470 complaints. This count does not include crank and psychiatric cases where the allegation was obviously unfounded, or those not dealing with local government activities. An initial assessment is made at the earliest stage of proceedings to weed out these types of grievances.

During the first six months of operation, approximately 175 complaints were received, compared to more then 300 in the second six month period. This increase is apparently attributable to the fact that the County Ombudsman is becoming more widely known throughout the community.

Chief users of the Ombudsman service to this point have been middle class complainants, perhaps because they are better informed by the various media of communication as to its existence. Judge Greason was of the opinion, however, that many less advantaged groups in the community will increasingly avail themselves of his office once it becomes known to them by word of mouth and example.

Complaint Handling—By far the greatest number of citizens direct their problem to the County Ombudsman by letter—in the neighborhood of 70 per cent compared to 20 per cent by telephone and 10 per cent by personal visit to his office. When a complaint is received, the customary practice is to direct a memorandum to the head of the County department concerned outlining the substance of the allegation and requesting a reply. The average time for the department's answer has been three days. Some cases require more extensive departmental investigation, but even in these cases a report normally has been returned to the Ombudsman within a week.

In many cases the complaint is relatively straightforward, and is often resolved on the spot by a telephone call to the appropriate authority. The telephone is also used when immediate or urgent action is necessary. For example, a woman reported that a neighbor's driveway was being asphalted by a County truck and workmen. Judge Greason telephoned the Commissioner of Public Works. Both the Commissioner and his Deputy rushed to the scene. They discovered an old truck previously hired by the County which had been sold to a purchaser in the construction industry who had left the County insignia on the truck. As the new owner did considerable work for the County, he was entitled under local law to retain the County insignia on the vehicle. But the work in progress was strictly a private undertaking. The Commissioner and his Deputy immediately knocked on the complainant's door and explained the situation to her complete satisfaction.

A few County employees have availed themselves of the Ombudsman to air grievances concerning their immediate superiors or working conditions. In these cases, Judge Greason has referred the complaint to the appropriate department head in the belief that the latter was probably unaware of the personnel difficulties within his administration and will correct them if feasible.

Anonymous complaints cannot be pursued in the usual manner, but they are not ignored. No departmental response to an anonymous complaint is required by the County Ombudsman. The substance of the grievance is directed to the department concerned for whatever action may be deemed appropriate. Justification for consideration of this type of complaint lies in the possible disclosure of a general situation requiring improvement.

Judge Greason has found that in most cases of administrative error or omission, the department head is unaware of the deficiency within his administration and is anxious to make corrections when informed of the situation. Not one administrator has refused to discuss a complaint with the Nassau County Ombudsman, and in very few cases has the latter been unable to cut the red tape of administrative bureaucracy. Even when a County department does not agree with the complainant's position, a hearing has almost always been granted the citizen to state his case even if he has already done so on an earlier occasion.

Jurisdictional Problems—Occasionally the County Ombudsman's jurisdiction to inquire into a matter is challenged. Under existing state legislation, home rule provisions place the two cities and the villages within Nassau County outside the scope of County government.

When a grievance concerns a city or village, Judge Greason does not throw up his hands in defeat. He transmits the details of the complaint to the appropriate city or village authority and requests an explanation. In these situations, it is not uncommon for a city or village official to preface his reply with a statement to the effect that the County Ombudsman has of course no jurisdiction to deal with the matter. However, in every case that same officer has then given the desired information and cooperated fully toward a resolution of the problem.

Another jurisdictional difficulty arises when a complaint falls within the sphere of federal or state activity. Again the Nassau County Ombudsman obviously has no power to act, but rather than simply decline to investigate, he refers the matter to the appropriate federal or state authority and follows up if necessary. Fourteen complaints involving the United States Government and thirty-nine dealing with New York

State Government were handled in this manner during the County Ombudsman's first year of operation.

These figures have given rise to the question whether an Ombudsman working on the local level should be vested with jurisdiction to handle problems arising out of federal and state administrative action on the local level. Generally speaking, a federal Ombudsman located in Washington has not been regarded as a feasible institution. If a federal Ombudsman operated on a decentralized basis however, and particularly at the local level, the Ombudsman institution might well prove appropriate for many federal government activities. The same holds true on the state government scene. Experience in Nassau County indicates that a local government Ombudsman might at least serve as a clearing house for grievances against federal and state administrative action.

An example of a more complicated nature was presented by a complaint of illegal dredging off the Long Island shore. Eight different federal, state and local government agencies were involved in the dispute. As a result of the Nassau County Ombudsman's intervention, a complete change in procedure was introduced to resolve the problem with the cooperation of all parties.

Non-Governmental Complaints—In 75 cases, government administration was not directly implicated at all. Again Judge Greason referred them to the appropriate body for attention.

Forty-six of these complaints concerned legal problems or services in one form or another. Greason reports that the legal profession has been most cooperative in handling complaints referred to it through the County Ombudsman's office. Undoubtedly his own judicial and professional background accounts to a considerable extent for the success in this area.

Of interest to most observers of the Ombudsman institution will be Judge Greason's handling of complaints against the judiciary. In these cases, he picked up the telephone and related the matter directly to the presiding judge of the appropriate court. The result is usually an informal talk between the presiding judge and his allegedly offending colleague in which the conduct giving rise to the complaint is discussed. Normally it concerns discourtesy toward a lawyer or witness, arrogance or a similar breach of courtroom decorum. This private and personal approach to the problem has proved effective. Greason justifies his intervention in the judicial sphere on the ground that respect for administration of justice is the keystone to an orderly democratic society. On the basis of his own experience and personal acquaintance with the judges of the courts, he is in a position to communicate with the judiciary to help avoid future breaches of judicial etiquette.

Disposition of Complaints—Judge Greason estimates that 20 per cent of complaints have proved to be valid, and almost all were resolved in a manner satisfactory to the parties concerned. This figure is substantially higher than usually experienced in the Scandinavian countries and New Zealand. One explanation offered by Greason is the accumulation of justified grievances which found an avenue of expression during the first year of the Nassau County Ombudsman operation.

Of the remainder, approximately 35 per cent were attributable to delay in the administrative process. In a sense, they were also valid complaints satisfactorily resolved by immediate attention to the situation. This type of grievance also opened the door to consideration of more efficient administrative procedures generally.

In the neighborhood of 45 per cent failed to disclose administrative error or ommission of any kind, but only 20 per cent of all complaints could be classified after investigation as completely unfounded. Even where the administrator's action was upheld, most complainants appeared satisfied with the explanation given by the County Ombudsman although they may have disagreed with the policy or result.

An example illustrating the extent to which the Nassau County Ombudsman will go above and beyond the call of duty concerned two orphans of a New York City family. The father had been deceased for quite some time and the mother in her thirties was dying of cancer, with no relatives on either side of the family. A neighboring couple with children of their own began taking care of the dying mother's children and continued to do so after her death. Financial strain occasioned by this additional burden on the Good Samaritan family caused them to move from New York City into Nassau County, but expenses continued to consume their meager savings. Having unsuccessfully made attempts to obtain assistance from Social Security, the discouraged couple took their problem to the Nassau County Ombudsman. Communication by his office with Social Security officials eventually yielded death benefits for the two children. Further investigation uncovered two bank accounts belonging to the natural parents and a trust fund for the children established by the mother before her death. As a result of these efforts, the new family unit is well on its way to financial recovery.

Some complaints lack substantial merit. For example, citizens in a certain neighborhood complained of governmental indifference toward a rodent menace. On investigation, it was discovered that only one rat had been sighted and it had been disposed of by a policeman called to the scene. Furthermore, conditions in the area were such as to attract the rodent population, and the complainants were chiefly responsible for this state of affairs.

Welfare and Police—Welfare problems have been of particular concern. In the first few months of operation, the volume of welfare complaints far exceeded those in any other area. This development appeared to be attributable to the complex nature of legislative and administrative checks to prevent abuse of the public purse by welfare recipients. These safeguards had produced a bureaucratic tangle in which the welfare claimant encountered immense difficulty in finding his way through the administrative maze. Faced with the large volume of inquiries being directed to him by the Ombudsman's office, the Nassau County Commissioner of Social Services charged one of his chief assistants with responsibility for facilitating communications with the County Ombudsman. A special effort by both the Social Services Department and the Ombudsman office is now being made to develop procedures for expeditious processing of complaints concerning welfare administration.

Only two complaints against law enforcement agencies have reached the Nassau County Ombudsman. In one case, a citizen had been convicted of a criminal offense and his case was on appeal when he resorted to the County Ombudsman alleging police brutality. Judge Greason asked the Chief of Police for a report on the matter and received complete cooperation. Greason concluded that the complaint lacked validity.

The second case concerned a suspect charged with distributing narcotics. He complained that on numerous occasions his apartment had been broken into by the police without a search warrant, and as a result he was being harassed by law enforcement authorities. When asked for an explanation, the head of the Narcotics Squad conducted an extensive investigation. Six policemen willingly stated that they had frequently visited the apartment of the accused, but that on each occasion he had voluntarily admitted them. However the Narcotics Squad agreed that searches of this kind and frequency would not be undertaken in the future.

Recommendations for Legislative Change—In some situations, Judge Greason has found the difficulty to lie in the area of legislative policy rather than administration. One problem concerned overweight and overlength trucks. Permits for travel of these vehicles on County roads over limited periods could be obtained by filing security bonds to cover repairs and other damage, but no comparable requirements existed for town roads. At Judge Greason's suggestion, a number of towns have passed ordinances with similar provisions.

Abuse of tax lien legislation is an outstanding example of the need for legislative change uncovered by the Nassau County Ombudsman. Under State and County laws, a lien for tax arrears on real property is sold by the County Treasurer to ensure tax collection. After expiry of a period fixed by law, usually two years, the lien holder is required to notify the property owner to pay the tax arrears. *Actual receipt* by the property owner of this notice to redeem, however, is not required under existing legislation. That the notice was mailed is sufficient. Unless the tax is then paid, a deed is given by the County Treasurer to the lien holder, and the original owner has lost his property.

Five separate cases have been brought to the County Ombudsman's attention in which the lien purchaser has confronted the original owner with the new deed and demanded payment of an exorbitant amount for it. For a variety of reasons, the original owners were unaware of the sale of the tax lien on their property. Apparently the purchase of tax liens has become a highly organized business in the County.

In one instance, a tax bill for $45 and the notice to redeem were not received by the original owner through no fault of his own. Yet the lien purchaser demanded $6,000 in settlement. Judge Greason discovered that the difficulty had been occasioned here by an incorrectly addressed notice to redeem. This made it possible to negotiate return of the property to the original owner for payment of the $45 plus interest. However, Judge Greason has recommended to the County Executive that County tax lien procedures be changed at the earliest possible opportunity to avoid similar abuses. A local law is being drafted to this end.

Conclusion—One year is too brief a period on which to base firm and lasting conclusions. So far, the utility and worth of an Ombudsman on the local level appears to be justified by the Nassau County experience. Although difficult to assess accurately, psychological benefits from the mere fact of the Ombudsman's existence are undoubtedly considerable. Nassau County's precedent is sufficiently encouraging to merit serious consideration by other communities.

CHICAGO

A new complaint center was established by the Office of Inquiry and Information of the City of Chicago in July 1966. Operating around the clock seven days a week, the service received approximately 2100 calls a day. The Chicago Daily News described it as "a Chicago counterpart, after a fashion, of the Scandinavian ombudsman."

Complaints are passed on to the appropriate city department with the aim of having each legitimate grievance corrected within 24 hours or as soon as possible thereafter. In reality, the Chicago complaint center would appear to be nothing more than an attempt to improve the reception of grievances by City Hall.

In a reorganization of the City Manager's office during the Spring of 1967, the San Diego City Council unanimously agreed to the creation of an assistant to the City Manager under the title of "Citizens Assistance Officer." This new outlet for irate citizens was described by the Los Angeles *Times* as "an 'ombudsman type' system." Where previously complaints were being answered by the city department which had stimulated them in the first place, the new office was empowered to receive and investigate complaints, rectify wrongs through the City Manager, and make recommendations to the City Council if necessary.

Although the Citizens Administrative Officer "will function somewhat as the ombudsman system in Scandinavian countries," he is not intended to supplant existing procedures or be regarded as a City Ombudsman.[13] He reports, and is responsible, to the City Manager. Most complaints are simply noted and referred to the appropriate City department asking for a reply. A courtesy call is subsequently made to the complainant to ascertain whether action has been taken to the latter's satisfaction.

Essentially the San Diego Citizens Assistance Officer is a watchdog overseeing the satisfactory handling of complaints by city departments. More serious complaints are directed to the City Manager for the attention of his immediate staff. Nevertheless the San Diego experiment is an interesting example of an attempt to improve complaint handling through an individual whose office is comparable in some respects to the Ombudsman institution.

HONOLULU

Under the City of Honolulu Charter, which became effective on July 1, 1959, provision was made for an Office of Information and Complaint attached to the Mayor's Office. Subsequent establishment of the Office of Information and Complaint discontinued separate information and public relations operations in various City departments. The Director of the Office also serves as an Administrative Assistant to the Mayor.

On receipt of a complaint, a "Request for Investigation & Service Report" is forwarded by the Office of Information and Complaint to the appropriate department "for full investigation, action and report," in the words of the Office's description of its function. In some cases, depending on the nature of the complaint, a preliminary investigation is first carried out by the Office's Complaint Investigator or In-

[13] Letter from San Diego City Manager Walter Hahn, Jr., to William H. Angus (July 7, 1967).

formation Specialist. A reply to the Office from the department concerned indicating the action to be taken is required within 20 days, followed by a further communication after the appropriate remedial steps have been completed. The complainant is then notified of the action taken or to be taken—or if none is contemplated, why this is so.

Honolulu's Office of Information and Complaint predates interest in transporting the Ombudsman concept to the United States scene. As an inside "City Hall" complaint service, the Office contains some Ombudsman characteristics but obviously it was not patterned on the Scandinavian institution.

The Buffalo Experiment

THE SETTING

With a population of 480,000, the City of Buffalo is the employment, commercial, financial, industrial, transportation and cultural center of the Niagara Frontier metropolitan region consisting of two counties (Erie and Niagara) and a population of about 1.3 million. It has New York State's greatest concentration of heavy industry, its second largest port, and the second largest railyards in the country. These characteristics are not unrelated to current political, economic and social problems which make Buffalo an excellent laboratory for an Ombudsman demonstration.

Development of Buffalo's port and rail facilities was attended by the growth of its flour milling and iron and steel production industries, which in turn influenced heavy immigration from Germany, Italy, Ireland and Poland in the late 19th and early 20th Century. The 1960 census breakdown of national origins of the people of Buffalo reveals a 9 per cent Polish element, 8 per cent Italian, and 5 per cent German. More recent immigration, originating directly or indirectly from the the South—and to a much smaller extent from Puerto Rico—has accounted largely for the increase in the number of non-whites in the City from 37,700 in 1952 to 83,946 in 1966. Resulting ethnic frictions and rivalries for political preferment, economic disparities, and social unrest have contributed to the labeling of Buffalo as a "problem city." Early in 1966, an Erie County Grand Jury was quoted in the Buffalo *Evenings News* as observing:

> Witness after witness, regardless of business or profession, testified with almost monotonous consistency that the City of Buffalo has a reputation, not only nationally, but internationally, of being an exceptionally rancorout [sic] city politically.

"Rancor" of another kind, though with political implications, was traumatically manifested in Buffalo's June, 1967, racial disturbances.

The problems of the affected Buffalo neighborhoods had already led to the recommendation that in Buffalo's application for a planning grant under the Demonstration Cities and Metropolitan Development Act of 1966, funds be sought to finance the establishment of an Ombudsman to help keep the people of those neighborhoods " 'from being victimized' in their many dealings with city officials, especially social service agencies." One version of the proposal would have located an Ombudsman, or representative of an Ombudsman, in each of a number of community service centers in the troubled areas. As an aftermath of the June episode, in the course of the search for solutions for the root problems giving rise to participation by unemployed youths in the disturbances, the Mayor was asked to create youth grievance centers in the neighborhoods to hear complaints and direct them to the Mayor.

Buffalo has a "strong mayor" form of city government. But vis-à-vis the Common Council, the Mayor's strength normally depends on the line-up of political affiliations of members of the two offices. In 1964 a Republican Mayor endorsed a resolution calling for the establishment by the Common Council of a Division of Complaints and Information in the Executive Department, modelled upon the complaint bureau operation in Philadelphia. The majority of the Council, Democrats, kept the proposal in committee where it died.

Acting on his own, the Mayor nevertheless established and operated a complaint bureau of sorts at City Hall over a period of about six months in 1965. It received over 5000 complaints, most of them relating to annoyances over alleged deficiencies in municipal services or unevenness in the exercise of municipal police power, such as the following: the maintenance of insanitary and hazardous conditions on vacant premises, particularly the sites of abandoned buildings; illegal parking; nuisances in city parks or other public places; violations of building ordinances and housing laws; leaks in city water lines; holes in street pavements; improper functioning of traffic regulation devices or personnel; violations of zoning ordinances; and damage to private property from city-owned trees.

Although the records of this operation indicate that the bulk of complainants were given prompt attention and a high percentage were given satisfaction, the venture was doomed to failure because it never received budgetary support from the Council. The complaint desk was manned by regular departmental personnel deputed to it for a week at a time on a rotating basis, hence could not provide adequate follow-through on complaints.

In the absence of a complaint bureau—and probably even when they had one—the residents of Buffalo have placed strong reliance on intervention of their Councilmen to get action from municipal agencies.

The efficiency of this method has varied from Councilman to Councilman. Even within a particular Councilman's jurisdiction it has varied from neighborhood to neighborhood—with variations sometimes explained as based on a lack of incentive to intercede for a neighborhood "that won't vote for me anyway," possibly because of ethnic factors.

Public health and social welfare are county functions in most of New York State. Welfare recipients offer the most abundant source of complaints against Erie County, in which Buffalo is located. The County Welfare Department has its own Adjustment Unit which may receive up to 1,500 complaints a month, most of them asserting late payment of benefits. Possibly the next largest category of gripes lodged with the County relates to public health, especially sanitation matters. Hence, it may turn out that while the activities of City government may engender the greatest variety of grievances, those of the County may yield the largest number.

ACTION LINES

A significant outlet for complaints against government on all levels appeared on the Buffalo scene early in 1967 when the *Buffalo Evening News* introduced a regular column entitled "Newspower." It holds itself out as "a forum for solving problems, getting action on complaints, correcting wrongs, cutting red tape, insuring your rights." A similar service shortly appeared in the competing *Buffalo Courier Express,* first as "Mr. Fixit," and then under the heading "Courier Action." Previously a television station had conducted an open line program by telephone, but this program had been discontinued before the newspaper columns commenced.

The *Houston Chronicle* inaugurated the newspaper action line in 1961, and its column continues to thrive. This success led to adoption of the idea by many of the nation's largest dailies. In the case of the *St. Louis Globe Democrat,* which guaranteed to answer all questions whether written or by telephone, the response required a staff of 19 to cope with the ensuing flood. Mounting costs soon compelled the *Globe Democrat* publishers to drop the column.

Telephone service brings a far greater number of queries, seemingly because people prefer to get the matter off their chest immediately by word of mouth rather than labor over a letter. To keep the number of questions within the capacity of the newspaper to handle them, many newspapers, including the *Buffalo Evening News* and *Buffalo Courier Express,* answer written questions only. As a result, however, less literate segments of the community are discouraged from addressing their queries or complaints to the action line columns.

A survey in Detroit, where the *Detroit Free Press* picked up 50,000 in circulation attributable to introduction of its action line column, indicated that 70 per cent of its readers consistently read this feature. Only the front page, comics and picture page normally reach that high a percentage.

Although not designed as an Ombudsman service, the action line column obviously is one to a considerable extent. In pursuit of journalistic objectives, its main purpose is to disseminate information. Only a small number of the total questions received can be answered by publication. These questions are hand-picked to achieve a number of goals, for example: as a guide for readers with similar problems; for news and human interest value; and for educational content.

Many of the questions simply seek information on obscure or difficult subjects. Others set forth specific complaints, many of them concerned with government administration. Illustrative of this mixture is the following breakdown of questions answered by the *Buffalo Evening News* action line column during the first six months of its existence (January 16, 1967 to July 15, 1967):

Subject Matter	Requests for Information		Complaints	
	Types	Number	Types	Number
Federal Government	26	95	11	34
State Government	33	91	24	63
Local Government	32	108	40	313
Total Government	91	294	75	410
Non-Governmental	80	269	25	95
Grand Total	171	563	100	505

Complaints relating to government exceeded those in the non-governmental area by more than 4 to 1, while requests for information about government matters only slightly exceeded non-governmental questions of this nature. Included in the non-governmental type of complaint are a substantial number directed to privately owned public utilities and services which come under government regulation.

Extremely interesting is the relatively large volume of complaints on the local government level. Mr. Elwood Wardlow, Assistant Managing Editor of the *Buffalo Evening News,* who is responsible for the "Newspower" column, states that the above figures fairly reflect the proportions of all questions and complaints received. Whether the explanation is greater efficiency on higher levels of government, or simply more volume and contact in matters of local government, is a matter of uncertainty. Probably a combination of many factors contributes to the situation.

Further analysis of the *Buffalo Evening News* action line for the first six months of its operation discloses the nature of complaints on the local government level:

Subject Matter	Number of Complaints
1. Road Repairs and Street Maintenance	43
2. Vacant Buildings and Land	33
3. Traffic Control	32
4. Trees	22
5. Parks and Recreation	20
6. Vehicle Parking	16
7. Sidewalks	16
8. Welfare	15
9. Littering	10
10. Public Utilities—Water and Sewage	10
11. Education	9
12. Hospitals and Homes	9
13. Public Buildings	8
14. Animals	7
15. Civil Service	6
16. Planning and Zoning	5
17. Police Administration	5
18. Building Violations	5
19. Miscellaneous (less than 5 complaints)	42
Total	313

This breakdown should be of considerable interest to those contemplating establishment of a municipal Ombudsman, because they reflect the variety of problems which will be directed to his office. The figures also give an accurate picture of the relative volume of all complaints received on each subject, according to Mr. Wardlow. Any community experiencing the usual symptoms of urban growth and decay can anticipate similar grievances. These problems seem very important and are annoying to citizens. Although many complaints clearly are not of overwhelming significance, attitudes to government and public administration are often shaped by reaction to handling of grievances on the local government level.

Most letters addressed to the "Newspower" service require substantial interpretation in order to determine the exact nature of the question or problem—a difficulty which an Ombudsman will also probably meet. Initially the flow of mail amounted to around 40 letters a day, but has gradually increased to about 80. Of these, approximately 30 present situations suitable for publication. Since the "Newspower" column ordinarily accomodates an average of 9 questions per day, a backlog accumulates. In many cases, however, answering one question will satisfy a number of inquiries.

In the beginning, no attempt was made to answer each correspondent individually. This policy, or lack of policy, occasioned considerable concern that an unanswered reader might be greatly troubled by the lack of response, and even take desperate action as a result. To remedy the problem, 23 form post cards were drafted to cover most all situations. In some instances where the query is directed to a particularly common subject, a lengthier printed answer is sent to the questioner. One post card simply says, in effect, "Sorry." This reply is sent when an answer cannot readily be provided, or when for policy reasons "Newspower" does not wish to deal with the matter. Close to 10 per cent of all "Newspower" correspondents receive "Sorry" for an answer. In every case, therefore, the person submitting the question or complaint now receives a reply by way of publication or a post card.

Most of the questions considered for publication require investigation. This task is performed through the desk of the City Editor by individual reporters or others on the newspaper staff. The person assigned to investigate also prepares both the question and answer for submission to the Assistant Managing Editor who is responsible for the content of "Newspower." A varied selection is then put together for daily publication.

Complaints against local government not regarded as suitable for publication are usually referred to the appropriate City or County department for whatever action it deems appropriate. A post card advising that the matter has been referred is always sent to the person who submitted the grievance. No follow up is carried out by "Newspower" unless the citizen complains that the referral failed to bring any action.

Clearly an action line column is not an Ombudsman, nor does it pretend to achieve the same results. Yet this service does resolve a limited number of complaints, while referrals to the appropriate governmental authorities undoubtedly satisfy many more grievances. Its great strength is the power of publicity, a resource on which the Ombudsman also relies when other avenues fail to yield results. In terms of informing and educating the public, the "Newspower" type of column has distinct advantages over the Ombudsman. Moreover it provides a valuable fund of information and experience relating to public administration, particularly on the local government scene. As a guide to governmental problems, the action line is a useful tool in the development of Ombudsman practices and procedures.

LOCAL GOVERNMENT OMBUDSMAN PROJECT

With the City of Buffalo offering a great variety of the local government problems plaguing urban areas in the United States today, the Law School of the State University of New York at Buffalo formulated plans for a local government Ombudsman project. Its objective was to experiment with application of the Ombudsman concept to the North American scene in a large urban setting.

Consent of the City of Buffalo authorities was readily obtained, a fact which may seem rather remarkable in view of the suspected propensity of city governments generally to close their doors to outside meddlers. Buffalo City officials took the sensible view that no corruption and little, if any, maladministration are present at City Hall. In their view, some inefficiency and delay might be discovered in certain departments, and if so, the men at the top would very much like to identify it so that remedial action could be taken. The only condition attached to the consent was that advance notice of critical findings be afforded the City administration in order to facilitate its own investigation and disposition of the matter in question. Customary Ombudsman practice is completely consistent with the City's one condition, which therefore presented no difficulty.

The City of Buffalo's commendable attitude reflects what is probably true of most local government administrations—that public officials are endeavoring to do their best, and often under very difficult circumstances. They are as anxious to please and improve their administrations as are citizens in the community. From its inception, the Buffalo Law School project has received the complete cooperation of City and County officials.

First Phase—For the initial portion of the experiment occupying the summer months of 1966, a few selected complaints were received through various organizations and individuals to be processed in Ombudsman fashion. A single Law School professor undertook this task. The object was solely to determine the feasibility of the Ombudsman principle in a voluntary situation. Corporation Counsel of the City promised to clear the way if any City official refused to cooperate. This eventuality did not arise, however, and officialdom seemed uniformly anxious to discuss the problems and relate their side of the story. In all instances, the allegations contained in the complaint were explained or resolved to the satisfaction of the parties concerned without proceeding beyond the particular department against which the grievance had been levelled.

Three examples will serve to illustrate the results of this first phase. An asphalt paved playground in a centrally located area of the

City contained various pieces of permanent equipment. Each autumn the removable portions were dismantled and stored for the winter months of unseasonable climate, to be installed the following spring. These detachable items were not reinstalled during the spring months of 1966, however, and numerous complaints had failed to produce them, nor had the playground area been cleaned up as usual. A visit by the acting Ombudsman to the Commissioner of the Parks Department produced the explanation that insufficient funds were responsible for failure to hire supervisors for a number of smaller playgrounds. Without supervision, damage to the equipment occurred and noise resulted in complaints from neighbors. The Commissioner advised that the detachable equipment would be reinstalled, however, if a responsible group would volunteer to supervise the play area. When this alternative was conveyed to the complainant, a neighborhood organization immediately volunteered to undertake the required supervision. As a result, the playground was cleaned up and the removable equipment returned, much to the delight of neighborhood children and parents in an area greatly in need of recreational facilities. The source of the difficulty in this case appeared to be a simple problem of communication between concerned citizens and civic authorities.

A second complaint dealt with an application for municipal housing by a woman in ill health. Her application had been refused because she did not meet the age qualification, nor did she fall within the category of disabled or handicapped persons for whom the age requirement could be waived. As these standards had been laid down by the Federal and State governments funding the public housing projects of the city, no exercise of administrative discretion could afford relief to the applicant despite her circumstances. Thus the Municipal Housing Authority had acted entirely properly. The difficulty arose either because the official who interviewed the applicant did not clearly explain the reasons for the rejection of her application, or the complainant did not fully comprehend the statutory limitations imposed on the housing authority.

Another grievance concerned a large vacant area in a residential section of the City. The property had been neglected by its owner, becoming a collecting place for trash, refuse and other material including an abandoned automobile. Subsequently the City acquired ownership of the land for nonpayment of taxes. As might be expected, children found the site an attractive play area. One particularly adventurous group became involved with the police and juvenile authorities when they pushed the abandoned automobile onto an adjoining railroad right of way. Complaints to the City had failed to remedy the situation. When the professor turned Ombudsman communicated with the Department of Street Sanitation, assurance was given that the matter would be investigated immediately. On the next day, the street in front of the property was swept clean of an accumulation of debris, but the vacant property remained as before. A personal visit to the Department to explain once again the exact nature of the problem brought remedial action within a day or two. One of the difficulties in this case appears to have been getting through to the proper City official or department. When word apparently reached the correct source, an undesirable state of affairs was corrected with commendable promptitude.

As a result of the favorable reaction of both City officials and complaining citizens to this first trial of the Ombudsman idea, a second and more extensive phase of the experiment was deemed desirable. Although extremely limited in scope, the first phase suggested that an Ombudsman might well be a useful addition to other means of local government complaint solving, even on a voluntary basis.

Second Phase—A Seminar on the Ombudsman was offered for credit to senior students in the Spring semester of 1967 as the second step in the project. Nine students enrolled, and after a preliminary study of the Ombudsman institution, were assigned complaints to process in Ombudsman fashion under supervision of the Seminar professor. Each student was required to interview the complainant; visit the site giving rise to the complaint, if necessary; investigate and confirm the facts; research the applicable statute or law; then meet with the appropriate local government department or officer to resolve the difficulty. A written report of his activities and their result concluded the assignment.

In addition to individual investigations, Seminar students were directed to research particular areas of grievance which appeared in the *Buffalo Evening News* action line column, to submit written solutions to problem complaints based on actual cases handled by the New Zealand Ombudsman, and to write a criticism of existing and proposed Ombudsman legislation.

Another aspect of the expanded second phase was the inclusion of the Erie County administration. The County Executive, being the chief elected County officer, had no hesitation whatsoever in agreeing to bring his administration within the experiment. Within the city boundaries of Buffalo, the County of Erie provides a number of key services, the most important from an Ombudsman viewpoint probably being the welfare field, owing to the quantity and complexity of its services.

Each student thoroughly investigated two or three complaints against

City or County governments. Local organizations and individuals were again relied on as sources since the limited resources of the project precluded opening it to the public at large. Although the quantity of problems was obviously insufficient as a basis for substantial conclusions, a reasonably wide sample was obtained by screening complaints before assigning them to the Seminar students.

One problem in the screening process is worth mentioning at this point. Many complaints did not relate to local government responsibities. At first these grievances were declined for the purposes of the experiment on the ground that they were beyond the purview of the project. As the experiment progressed, however, it became clear that many federal and state matters are administered on the local level, and probably could be handled without undue inconvenience. To test this further, a few selected grievances relating to federal and state activities were accepted and processed in the usual manner. These cases presented no greater difficulty in terms of operation of the experiment than those dealing with local government situations, although none went beyond the local field offices of federal and state administration.

Again, a few examples of complaints encountered and their resolution will serve best to illustrate the working of the project's second phase. Buffalo has many vacant old frame houses which are fire, child and health hazards. Local laws authorize the City to order a citizen to repair or demolish these buildings, and on failure to comply, the City may effect the repairs or demolition and recoup by billing the owner or filing a lien against the property. A group of complainants asserted that the City had failed to take action to demolish a particular building despite their protests. On investigation, it turned out that City authorities had been actively pursuing the proper demolition procedures, and crews were scheduled to commence removing the eyesore within a few days. These procedures are usually lengthy owing to the necessity of preserving the owner's interest in his private property, the requirement of public tenders on the demolition, and the subsequent work scheduling by the winning bidder. Although numerous complaints had been received by various City departments about the structure in question, they went unacknowledged while the standard demolition procedure took its usual course. Some form of communication to the complainants that the matter was in hand would undoubtedly have gone a long way towards easing their fears concerning apparent City inaction to meet the abandoned building hazard in this instance. Undoubtedly the same holds true as a general rule where a time lapse necessarily intervenes between the filing of a complaint and governmental action to remedy it.

Another noteworthy complaint was registered against the County Welfare Department by a citizen who claimed that his welfare payments were inadequate and less than the amounts to which he was entitled. Investigation disclosed that the aggrieved individual had received substantial sums from the Welfare Department for the repair and maintenance of his house, for a cottage on the same lot rented to another welfare client, and for his monthly mortgage payments. The Welfare Department expressed itself as willing to listen to any further request for assistance, including the cost of demolishing the dilapidated cottage. It was clear, however, that the Welfare Department was already treating this complainant in a generous manner.

An adoption case presented problems of considerable difficulty. A couple in their fifties became emotionally attached to a one-year-old child placed in a nearby foster home. The Foster Child Care Unit caseworker led them to believe that they might be able to adopt this particular child. Consequently they made the necessary application to do so. After considerable confusion and delay owing to the intervention of the summer vacation period, they were interviewed at the adoption office by a Home Finding Unit caseworker who, because of an administrative omission, had no previous knowledge of their association with the particular child in question. Further complications developed because the hopeful couple were adjudged to be too old to adopt a very young child, and the religion of the prospective parents was not the same as that of the child's natural parents. When the child was placed for adoption elsewhere, the hopeful couple were understandably distressed. The adoption service was equally upset in this awkward situation, but felt that the best interests of the child were the paramount factor. To prevent future situations of this nature, the adoption service voluntarily instituted three specific changes in departmental procedure. When the complaint finally reached the Citizens Administrative Service (as the project is called) of the Law School, obviously nothing could be done to bring about adoption of the child by the complainants. However the mystery which had surrounded the whole proceeding was dispelled by frank and open disclosure on the part of the adoption service. When a detailed explanation was communicated to the complainants by the Service, they expressed satisfaction that at last the facts behind the situation had been disclosed to them.

Third Phase—Completion of the second phase has set the stage for a trial run open to the public. A grant by the Office of Economic Opportunity will permit a one year operation commencing in the autumn of 1967. Hopefully it will yield significant results in the form of carefully planned research and valuable experience for establishment of municipal Ombudsman operations in other urban communities.

Allocation of Informational, Legal and Grievance Functions

It is predictable that pressures will be exerted to convert an American municipal Ombudsman into a multi-function officer—one compelled to give information, conduct investigations, render assistance, and criticize and advise local governments. Yet it is also predictable that he cannot develop into a complete municipal complaint bureau, commission of investigation and neighborhood handyman, and at the same time do a responsible job of promoting administrative reform.

The problem is one of balance, and its solution will require the fashioning of intricate arrangements between the Ombudsman and other agencies of local government for allocating to them the major responsibilities for performing the more routine, less ombudsmanic functions. He must be prepared to give some information, conduct some investigations, and render some assistance. But it is unrealistic to suppose that in Buffalo, for instance, he could supplant the Adjustment Unit of the County Welfare Department, which processes 1,500 complaints of welfare recipients each month. It is equally obvious that he cannot become the chief investigative officer in every matter of asserted venality of officers or breakdown in municipal services. He cannot be a substitute for the supervisory personnel in the streets, sanitation and police departments in disciplining the civil servants under their command; he can only criticize the methods by which they discharge these responsibilites, and possibly offer constructive criticism leading to procedural improvements. That is the conclusion reached by Professor Gellhorn in *When Americans Complain:*

> Responsibility for investigation belongs to the supervisory ranks of the administration itself. The external critic's concern should be less with the merits of the particular grievance than with the adequacy of the steps taken to discover what merit it has . . .
> The administrator tries the facts; the critic tries the administrator.

This means that in a city like Buffalo, the ultimate success of an Ombudsman would be measured in terms of his influence in promoting the re-establishment of an efficient complaint bureau at City Hall, and the smooth functioning of complaint-handling apparatus in the County Welfare Department.

To be sure there are more sensitive citizen-official relationships than those arising from the performance of rubbish removal or street repair functions. Can the municipal Ombudsman work out a *modus operandi* with the local police chief regarding perhaps the most sensitive area of all, the treatment of alleged abuses by police personnel? In the absence of American experience, we can only speculate on the subject. It is conceivable that given a cooperative mayor and police commissioner, or county executive and sheriff, a satisfactory working relationship might be developed with the local Ombudsman. At the very least the Ombudsman should be free to spot check grievance procedures of the police department. It should be clearly understood that the function of the Ombudsman would not be to supersede the police authorities in preferring or trying charges against police personnel. But by investigating particular cases, perhaps on the basis of selected complaints, he could familiarize himself with the techniques by which, in some cases, the affected citizen derives ultimate redress—through vindication by punishment of offending policemen.

The Ombudsman walks a tightrope here. If disciplinary procedures are loaded in favor of the alleged police offender in general, or in particular instances, the Ombudsman may criticize them, and possibly suggest procedural reforms. But he cannot alter the decision in any given disciplinary proceeding, any more than he may overrule any other type of administrative decision.

Jurisdictional Problems

That era of American local government in which municipal jurisdiction and municipal functions were easily identified and closely correlated is drawing to a close. Government administration specialists and lawmakers are promoting greater flexibility in local government structure and relationships, and inventing new techniques for inter-local cooperation and transfers of function. "Intergovernment," "multi-government," and "shared functions" are coming to be "in" words in the literature of local government, reflecting the increasing importance of federal and state roles in what were once purely local concerns, ranging from street construction to smoke abatement. The problem of delineating the area and subject jurisdiction of the municipal Ombudsman becomes correspondingly complex.

A dilemma is posed. The objects of citizens' complaints are not all stationed at city hall. They may be county, state or federal agencies, or possibly semi-autonomous bodies like public authorities. If all or some are put beyond the reach of a municipal Ombudsman, his ability to serve local citizens would be seriously curtailed, and the public might soon become disenchanted with the Ombudsman concept. For instance, an Ombudsman operating within the City of Buffalo would be drastically reduced in stature and effectiveness if he were just a "city Ombudsman" and had to turn away all complaints addressed to the County Welfare Department (a few blocks away) or the County Health Department (located within City Hall). Yet, as suggested above, an Ombudsman appointed by the state legislature would be neither "municipal" nor an "Ombudsman." And the struggle in Nassau County attests to the difficulty of an Ombudsman not appointed by the county governing board, but exercising jurisdiction over city and town officials within the county.

As a way out of the dilemma, in prescribing the Ombudsman's territory and official concerns the crucial consideration should be the number of people, size of the area, and identification of the "community" he is to serve, not the character of the particular appointing body. Given population and territory of optimum size, coinciding with an identifiable community (say, in the Buffalo area, all or the major part of Erie County), the problem of providing for the Ombudsman's appointment can then be defined in rational terms, and if necessary, special techniques can be devised. For instance, all, or the major, units of government operating within the given area might enter into a cooperative Ombudsman enterprise much as they now engage in the performance of joint or cooperative services. They might establish a joint representative body with the limited functions of appointing the Ombudsman and dismissing him for cause.

Other alternatives will readily come to mind, such as a joint appointment in the first instance by designated legislative or executive officials (or a mix of both) from the municipalities and public authorities concerned. The Ombudsman's traditional powers would be exercised with respect to all agencies of the participating municipalities. With respect to federal and state matters, he would act as a referral and, to some extent, information agency.

The establishment of "Little City Halls" in New York City reflects a trend towards decentralization of local government services, especially social services. Experience with anti-poverty programs has taught urban scientists that for one reason or another—inadequate public transportation, or the inability of the citizen to leave his employment or domestic responsibilities during regular city hall hours, to name just two—social services must be brought to the people. New York City's Commissioner of Investigation and the architects of the Buffalo demonstration Ombudsman project have anticipated that to be effective, the municipal Ombudsman will have to operate out of neighborhood offices.

If the Ombudsman's territory should cover rural government, such as towns and villages or outlying cities within a metropolitan jurisdiction or county, the problems of accessibility may be multiplied. Should the Ombudsman have field representatives in rural areas? Should he rely on existing governmental agencies, such as town clerks, to serve as repositories for complaints? Should he dispatch a mobile office or circuit-riding assistant to the boondocks?

The volume and nature of grievances from citizens in sparsely settled portions of the Ombudsman's domain may not justify the expense of special complaint receiving or complaint handling apparatus, as it might in the urban neighborhood. The experience of Scandinavian Ombudsmen with authority over local acts indicates that a central office in the core city might suffice in most situations. In the absence of actual experience, based on trial and error, further conjecture on the point cannot be meaningful.

Conclusion

As a testing ground for establishment of the Ombudsman in the United States, local government offers distinct advantages. Already the first working approximation has appeared in Nassau County, and the Buffalo project should provide further insight into the institution's applicability to the American scene. Many other communities are considering similar proposals. Relative ease in passing local enabling legislation may give rise to a number of municipal Ombudsmen before implementation of the idea on federal and state levels. Widespread exposure of the institution in many communities should ensure a rich variety of results.

Two caveats should be entered at this point. Danger exists that indiscriminate use of the "Ombudsman" label and proliferation of his functions may soil his reputation. Care must be taken to ensure that the Ombudsman institution in the United States does not degenerate into just another complaint bureau.

Nor should the Ombudsman be regarded as a cure-all. He may correct some wrongs in individual cases, but the institution will be truly effective only if government administration is encouraged thereby to develop its own procedures for efficient resolution of complaints. Existing avenues in the American system for remedy of administrative error and abuse will continue to occupy a place of prime importance.

To recapitulate, grievances on the local government level may seem trivial compared to federal and state fields of public administration. Nevertheless, these relatively small issues are of substantial importance to the complaining citizen. They arise more frequently, and touch him more closely. His attitude to government in general is largely shaped by his experience with local authorities. Thus the present experiments with local government Ombudsmen are of critical importance on the American scene.

Stanley V. Anderson

5

Proposals and Politics

Upsurge of interest in the Ombudsman idea has been fantastic, extending even to the international sphere where Professor Frank calls attention to "three treaty proposals—the Civil and Political Rights Covenant, its accompanying Protocol, and the Convention on Racial Discrimination—[in which] the United Nations have constructed two committees that could serve powerfully as ombudsmen for worldwide human rights." [1] The spread of other adoptions and proposals outside the United States is chronicled in Chapter 1. In Chapter 4, Professors William Angus and Milton Kaplan catalogue partial implementations in Buffalo, Chicago, Honolulu, Nassau and San Diego, and actual legislative proposals for local American Ombudsmen in Kansas City, New York City, Oakland, Philadelphia and Washington, D.C. Serious interest by prominent political leaders and others has been expressed as well in Baltimore, Cincinnati, Hartford, St. Louis, and San Francisco. No systematic survey has been carried out, and the list is undoubtedly incomplete.

At the state level, the rate of increase of proposals from year to year is even more impressive. Connecticut was alone in considering Ombudsman legislation in 1963. In 1965, that state was joined by California, Illinois, Massachusetts, New York and Utah. Alaska, Michigan, New Jersey and Rhode Island came along in 1966. With the partial exception of Utah, each state has continued to entertain proposals at successive sessions. By 1967, bills had been dropped in the legislative hopper of half the states, stretching from Florida to Washington and Maine to California, and in Puerto Rico. Many states have more than one bill, and most bills have more than one author.

[1] Frank C. Newman, "Ombudsmen and Human Rights: The U.N. Treaty Proposals," *The University of Chicago Law Review, 34,* No. 4 (Summer, 1967), 959.

Congressman Henry S. Reuss has reintroduced his proposal for an Administrative Counsel of Congress every two years since 1963, most recently as H.R. 3388 at the 1967 Session. In the latter year, Senator Edward V. Long offered his own bill, S. 1195, for the creation of an Administrative Ombudsman.

Yet, of all the American jurisdictions, only one deliberative body has actually enacted an Ombudsman bill. The Legislature of the State of Hawaii passed a measure creating the office of Ombudsman at the 1967 Session. The Ombudsman Act became law in June, upon expiration of the time within which the Governor could exercise his veto, and without his signature. Even this enactment, then, is under the shadow of executive dubiety. And, as the legislature had adjourned before the measure came into force, no appointment or appropriation can be made before 1968. Selection of an Ombudsman by joint session of the two Houses may not be speedy; they took seven years to agree upon a Legislative Auditor. Moreover, the Ombudsman question may be examined anew at the 1968 State Constitutional Convention.

After one has shown the increase in interest in Ombudsman to be concomitant with the growth of bureaucracy, as Professor Donald C. Rowat does in Chapter 1, and having shown potential gains from adoption to far outweigh potential losses, as Professor William B. Gwyn does in Chapter 2, one might well express surprise not at the number of proposals but at the paucity of adoptions. Why have not more of these proposals become law?

The Political System

Democracy is the right of the people to make mistakes—a privilege which is reserved to more select groups under other political systems. In representative democracy, the people delegate this competence to their elected surrogates. Constitutional systems limit the kinds of mistakes which the people or their representatives are permitted to make. For one thing, they are not allowed to make the mistake of restricting the future exercise of the right to make mistakes; thus, freedom of belief, speech, press and assembly may not be impaired. We have a system, then, of limited delegated popular trial and error. As the trial-and-error system obviously includes both error and trial, it is fair to ask: how does one get a trial? To put it more concretely, when all the speculation and prognostication is concluded, how does one get the people to give the office of Ombudsman a try?

Following the ponderous techniques of direct democracy, one could attempt constitutional amendment, or, where permitted by the constitution, popular initiative. In Sweden, Finland and Denmark, provision for Ombudsman was included in the basic laws of 1809, 1919, and 1953, respectively, and this is the approach currently being taken in Guyana and Mauritius. More commonly, however, using indirect democracy, one would seek the requisite majority in the legislative chambers and the consent of the chief executive. But legislative enactment is the last step in the decision to try an institutional experiment. First, a bill has to be introduced, and then it has to overcome the numerous roadblocks to passage which our suspicious forebears have erected. Apart from the obvious procedural formalities, how does one get a bill introduced and guided through to final adoption by a legislature?

INSTITUTIONAL SETTING

The Commonwealth countries and Scandinavia are characterized by parliamentarism and strong party discipline. A Cabinet is put into office by a majority of the members of Parliament, and it directs that majority—if necessary, by use of "the Whip"—to the enactment of Government policy. (The process is more complex and the outcome less certain when the Government is based upon a coalition of parties, or when it has only minority support and mere majority toleration.)

In these countries, then, to get an Ombudsman, one must convince a Government of its potential worth. Where, as in Britain, New Zealand and the Canadian provinces, the Government is composed of a single majority party, one must convince that party. It seems, however, that the leaders of a political party are more receptive to reform proposals when they are in Opposition as a minority. Having put forward a proposal as a plank in a campaign platform, the leaders will be compelled by consistency to continue to espouse and even possibly to enact the proposal when they have become a Government.

This indeed was the course of events for the adoption of Ombudsman in New Zealand and Great Britain. While standing as Opposition to the Labor Government, the National Party in New Zealand promised an Ombudsman if it were victorious in the 1960 elections. After winning a majority of seats in the unicameral Parliament, the National Party leaders formed a Government which consequently introduced (1961) and implemented (1962) an Ombudsman Act. Similarly but conversely in Britain, the Labor Party while in Opposition to the Conservatives included the Ombudsman as an election pledge in 1964. As described in Chapter 1, this led to the establishment of a Parliamentary Commissioner in 1967.

In Alberta, on the other hand, the Government became convinced of the wisdom of Ombudsman while in office, and moved quickly to bring a proposal to fruition in 1967. With heavy majorities, the Social Credit Party has formed the provincial Government continuously since 1935.

Happily for the later effective operation of the Ombudsman office, essential majority support need not entail minority disapproval because, to repeat an earlier observation, minority parties seem to be more receptive to suggestions for reform—and particularly when the reform happens to be a new means of control of government. The upshot is that new Ombudsman offices are created by consensus. This was true in Great Britain and New Zealand. In multi-party systems, consensus is a more direct prerequisite for adoption, and was forthcoming in the enactment of Ombudsman legislation in Denmark (1954) and Norway (1962).

So, we have reduced the earlier question of introduction and enactment to one of the crystallization of consensus. Before asking how the consensus is formed, we should take a brief look at our own system of government.

Government in the United States is characterized by presidentialism and weak party discipline. The executive and legislative branches are separately elected for fixed terms, and one cannot assume an identity of interest between them. What the Congress or state legislature enacts, the President or Governor may veto, subject to being overridden; what the chief executive espouses may not be enacted.

Having bifurcated power, we fragment it through the absence of party cohesion. Political parties lack central agencies to choose candidates, finance campaigns, and discipline mavericks. Within federal and state legislatures, the decisions of party caucuses are infrequent and not binding. (City Councils are at least ostensibly non-partisan.)

In contrast, then, to the neatness of the parliamentary systems, we see a continual jockeying for power in each of two legislative houses, rivalry between them, and competition by them with the executive. Cutting across this maelstrom is the conflict of the political parties. In Canada or Britain, when the Government wants to move ahead, it can demand right of way. In the United States, proposals—such as for an Ombudsman—must wait at each intersection for the signal of sometimes capricious policemen.

Yet some measures move smoothly to enactment. Generally speaking this can happen either through partisan push—where one party controls all of the intersections—or by consensus pull. Because the Ombudsman must rely upon persuasion rather than coercion, it is important that he come into being by consensus, or at least toleration, and not in the face of strong partisan opposition. Just as with our neighbors, then, the question of introduction and enactment is transformed into one of the engineering of consensus.

LEGITIMIZATION

Ideologically, the Ombudsman idea does not lend itself to monopolization by either party. To a great extent, each has accepted the growth of government. Democrats favor governmental intervention whenever it can be shown to be beneficial; Republicans oppose it unless it can be shown to be beneficial. Overlap is far greater than disparity. Both, then, are prone to foster devices which reduce annoyance and ameliorate occasional harshness or unfairness of government. The Ombudsman purports to be such a device. The broad spectrum of support described in Chapter 2, then, is not surprising.

In practice, Ombudsman proposals in the United States have not acquired a partisan hue. The author of the first state Ombudsman proposal was a Republican, Nicholas Eddy, Assistant Majority Leader in the 1963 Connecticut House of Representatives. Mr. Eddy viewed his bill, H.B. 3891/1963, as a partisan reform measure. Yet, when he retired from politics in 1967, one of the seven authors of the five bills which replaced his was a Democrat. More strikingly, the initial companion Ombudsman proposals in the New York State Legislature were authored by Republican Assemblyman S. William Green (A.B. 2105/1965) and Democratic-Liberal Senator Jack E. Bronston (S.B. 2692/1965).

Taking the state proposals as a whole, sponsorship has been more often joint than exclusive. Where the authors have all come from the same party, it has more frequently been Democratic than Republican. The groundswell of proposals at all levels has been spontaneous, and, as Professor Walter Gellhorn puts it, "without the assistance of any organization of spreaders." [1]

Just as with authorship, support and opposition have cut across party lines. In Hawaii, for example, the successful bill, S.B. 19/1967, was introduced by State Senator Duke Kawasaki, a Democrat. Twelve other Democrats joined Senator Kawasaki as co-authors. Twenty Democrats joined in introducing companion measures in the House of Representatives. Yet, in the Senate—a chamber composed of 15 Democrats and 10 Republicans—the proposal was passed by a vote of 23 to 1. The lone dissenter was a Democrat. In the House, where the bill passed 38 to 12, opposition was led by Republican Katsugo Miho. But Governor John A. Burns, who allowed the proposal to become law without his signature, is a Democrat.

Zealous conversion to the idea of Ombudsman has been personal

[1] Letter dated April 20, 1967.

rather than political. Ralph Nader inspired the initial Republican proposal in Connecticut and, two years later, the proposal in the Illinois General Assembly whose prime mover was a Democrat, Nader's law school classmate Harold A. Katz. The proposal, H.B. 1772/1965, had bipartisan authorship. Leadership on the Senate side was picked up in 1967 by President *pro tem.* W. Russell Arrington, a Republican.

In California, Speaker Jesse M. Unruh had agreed to intervene on behalf of a disgruntled bank franchise seeker; before he could do so, the supplicant was indicted for a massive theft. Had Speaker Unruh acted promptly, his political career might have come to an abrupt end. Sober realization of the dangers of intervention, then, gave Mr. Unruh a poignant appreciation of the need for legislators to have an impartial and expert office to which they might refer grievances.

Too impatient to wait for colleagues to come around of their own accord, proponents become proselytizers. To win acceptance, however, they need generate only acceptance, not enthusiasm. The stimulation of widespread approval of an idea may be designated as legitimization. To be legitimized, an idea must first become familiar. Ironically, debate on the merits of an issue may provide the basis for the familiarity which is a precondition of legitimacy. Opponents of the idea of Ombudsman, then, can hardly publicize their disapproval without adding to familiarization. Every assertion about the Ombudsman posits the existence of the institution and implies that it is at least worthy of attention, if not of support. The catchy exoticism of the name "Ombudsman" has greatly facilitated the generation of familiarity.

In spite of the efforts of Hollywood press agents and Madison Avenue hucksters—experts in the art of familiarizing—there is still a difference between fame and notoriety. For an idea to become legitimate, it must not only be broadcast, but it must be justified. Justification is an exercise in the art of rational persuasion. (Coincidentally, this is also the art which an Ombudsman practices in the function of his office.) Persuasion is a two-way street. It implies dialogue in which either or any of the participants may modify his position. Commonly, the idea in contention is changed to meet valid objections.

Almost anyone who wants to can join the ranks of the opinion-makers, by working through an appropriate organization; the price of being influential is persistent hard work. Subtle but pervasive social norms define the groups which are permitted to participate importantly in the dialogue of persuasion. These include elected officials, the media of communication, experts, and the representatives of those who are particularly affected by the subject in question. The last are, of course, pressure groups; their representatives are lobbyists. In our pragmatic society, a good deal of the dialogue of persuasion concerns "squeaking wheels." Lobbyists bring the squeak, or the potential friction, to the legislators' attention.

To return to the question which began this section, how does one get the people to give the office of Ombudsman a try? The answer is, by publicity and reasoned persuasion. The two are intertwined, and the level of argument may range from simple to subtle. The catalogue of potential advantages and disadvantages so carefully organized and analyzed in Chapter 2, for example, may be distorted by advocacy so that a single possible benefit or a particular feared drawback is given exaggerated or even exclusive attention.

The Unruh Proposal

California provides a good case study of the role of legitimization in the politics of adoption of Ombudsman. Publicity and attempted persuasion have been extensive, and are by no means concluded. Indeed, they will doubtless continue even after the office is created.

In 1963, the Institute of Governmental Studies on the Berkeley campus of the University of California started an Ombudsman project under the supervision of Stanley Scott, Acting Director. The present author was brought in as consultant early in 1964. In addition to bibliographical research,[2] the Institute has directed its attention to the adequacy of existing avenues of remedy for citizens' grievances— specifically, the role of the Governor and of state legislators in handling complaints.

Interest in the Ombudsman was stimulated in the late summer of 1964 by a short visit from Sir Guy Powles, the New Zealand Ombudsman, who stopped in San Francisco on his way home from the Montreal meetings of the Canadian Bar Association. Among those with whom he consulted were members of the Center for the Study of Democratic Institutions. At the headquarters of the Center in Santa Barbara, roundtable discussions on the Ombudsman were held both before and after Sir Guy's interview, and have continued since from time to time, in 1966, for example, in connection with the visit of the Israeli State Comptroller, Dr. I. E. Nebenzahl. Center President Robert M. Hutchins has made the Ombudsman an occasional theme in his syndicated column.

The New Zealand Ombudsman also talked with representatives of the Institute of Governmental Studies and the Northern California

---

[2] The Institute's bibliography is incorporated in Charles L. Smith, ed., *The Ombudsman: A Bibliography* (Friends Committee on Legislation of California, February 1965; 2nd. ed., March, 1966).

Friends Committee on Legislation. The interest of the Center, the Institute, and the Quakers was only prologue to that of the State's political leaders. Several members of Governor Edmund G. Brown's staff were intrigued by the Ombudsman idea, particularly in the Program and Policy Office of the Department of Finance, which is the Governor's research arm. Governor Brown's Executive Secretary, Winslow Christian, cooperated with the Institute in permitting a study of complaint mail flow during the month of July, 1965.[3]

The first real breakthrough for the practicability of the adoption of an Ombudsman in California came with its espousal by Assembly Speaker Jesse M. Unruh. On January 28, 1965, Speaker Unruh introduced House Resolution No. 100, which proposed to set up a "Citizens Advisory Study Committee on the office of Ombudsman," composed of "nine members appointed by the Speaker . . . from appropriate academic, legal, and administrative fields." The Committee was to report to the Legislature by January, 1967.

The Citizens Advisory Committee was never formed. It was superseded by Assembly Bill 2956, proposing the creation of an Ombudsman office, which was introduced by Assemblyman Unruh on April 22, 1965. With the recommendation "Do pass" from the Committees on Government Organization and Ways and Means, respectively, the Bill reached the floor of the Assembly on June 8, 1965. It had been amended to include Assemblyman Winfield A. Shoemaker as co-author, and to provide for an appropriation of $265,000. Senator Alvin C. Weingand became Senate sponsor. All three authors are Democrats. Accompanying A.B. 2956 on third reading was an initially inadvertant recommendation from the Governor—also a Democrat—certifying the measure as an "emergency" matter, so that it could be considered prior to enactment of the Budget Bill.

After a protracted call of the House, during which absent members were escorted to the locked chamber, A.B. 2956 passed by a roll-call vote of 54 to 20—a substantial majority, but barely two-thirds of the total membership of 80 which is required for measures containing appropriations. During the call, the Speaker's staff assistants were busy soliciting support. Suffering from an inflamed knee injured in a basketball game, Speaker Unruh was absent.

The proposal was sponsored by Democrats, as already noted, and support for it came primarily from that party, while Republicans voted against the measure at a ratio of two to one. Still, support and opposition were found in both parties, as can be seen in the following chart.

[3] See Gerald R. MacDaniel, *et. al.*, *Letters of Complaint: Mail-Processing in California's Administrative Branch* (University of California, Berkeley: Institute of Governmental Studies, 1967), discussed in Chapter 3, above.

Vote on A.B. 2956, June 8, 1965

	Aye	No	Not Voting	Total
Democrats	45	2	2	49
Republicans	9	18	4	31
Total	54	20	6	80

Assembly Bill 2956 was sent to the Senate, where it was referred to the Committee on Governmental Efficiency. On June 14, 1965, the Bill was presented to the Committee by Senator Weingand. Consistently with its record as a graveyard for reform, the Governmental Efficiency Committee rejected the proposal, on a voice vote, but accepted Weingand's suggestion that it be sent to interim study.

Mr. Unruh gave evidence of his continuing sponsorship of Ombudsman legislation in California in a number of speeches and in an article in the *California Law Review*.[4] Two public hearings on his proposal were held by the Assembly Interim Committee on Government Organization, chaired by Assemblyman (now State Senator) Milton Marks, a Republican. The first was held in Sacramento on March 1, 1966, to hear the testimony of Judge Alfred Bexelius, the Swedish Ombudsman. The second took place in Los Angeles on September 26, 1966. With the Speaker leading off, a number of legislators and scholars gave arguments for a California Ombudsman. The Southern California branch of the American Civil Liberties Union also expressed support.

Meanwhile, as described in Chapter 3, the Institute of Governmental Studies placed interns in the local offices of several state legislators.[5] The Section on Administration of Justice of the Commonwealth Club of California held several Sessions on the subject of Ombudsman during 1965 and 1966. Redress of citizen grievances in urban areas was the subject of a two-day conference in Los Angeles—attended by Speaker Unruh—sponsored by the Institute for Local Self Government and the Institute of Governmental Studies, and organized by the Institute's former Executive Director, Randy Hamilton.[6]

[4] "The Need for an Ombudsman in California," *California Law Review, 53*, No. 5 (December, 1965), 1212-13, reprinted as an appendix in U.S. Congress, Senate, Committee on the Judiciary, Subcommittee on Administrative Practice and Procedure, *Ombudsman* (March 7, 1966), pp. 334-35.

[5] See Dean E. Mann, *Complaint Handling by State Legislators in California* (University of California, Berkeley: Institute of Governmental Studies, 1967).

[6] See Randy Hamilton, ed., *A Preliminary Inventory of Selected Administrative Procedures for the Redress of Citizen Grievances in California's Urban Areas* (Berkeley: Institute for Local Self Government, 1966). The Institute is the research arm of the League of California Cities.

On March 13, 1967, Speaker Unruh reintroduced his bill, with a few minor changes, as A.B. 1020. Democratic Senator Mervyn M. Dymally sponsored a companion measure. Assemblyman Shoemaker remained co-author, joined by Democratic Assemblymen March K. Fong and Harvey Johnson. As in 1965, the Bill was referred to the Committee on Government Organization, of which Assemblyman Johnson was the new Chairman. After favorable consideration by this committee, and by the Assembly Committee on Ways and Means, the proposal was sent to the plenary body. As provision for appropriation had been deleted, an absolute majority, 41 votes, was sufficient for passage. Again, a call of the House was necessary, but this time only twenty minutes were needed to bring members from their offices and "to work on the floor." With a single vote to spare—42 to 32—the Unruh proposal was sent on to the Senate on May 31.

Vote on A.B. 1020, May 31, 1967

	Aye	No	Not Voting	Total
Democrats	37	0	5	42
Republicans	5	32	1	38
Total	42	32	6	80

Compared with 1965, there was an increased tendency toward Republican solidarity in opposing the Bill, as can be seen in the chart above. Mr. Unruh found this regrettable, as he does not consider the proposal to be partisan. Only two Assemblymen changed their 1965 votes; one Democrat switched from "no" to "aye," while one Republican went from "aye" to "no." Only part of the 14 additional Republican negative votes can be attributed to the fact that they increased their number in the Assembly by seven. Five Republicans who voted for the Ombudsman in 1965 were no longer members of the Assembly in 1967. Of the five who did vote for the measure in 1967, three were carryovers from 1965, while two were freshmen.

This time, the Bill hobbled on for an additional step in the Senate before suffering the same fate it had met two years before. At the urging of State Senator Alan Short, and under the gavel of President pro Tempore Hugh M. Burns—both Democrats—the Committee on Governmental Efficiency allowed the measure to move out, but without recommendation. On August 1, 1967, the final axe was wielded by the Senate Committee on Finance, chaired by Democrat George Miller, Jr. As a softening gesture, the Committee approved the motion of Mr. Burns (who serves on both committees) to refer the matter for further interim study. In connection with this and other proposals which died in the Senate, Speaker Unruh excoriated that body for its narrowness of vision. He remains convinced, however, "that through persistence the logic of an Office of Ombudsman for the State of California will be realized." [7]

There is some chance that an Ombudsman proposal will be supported by Republican Governor Ronald Reagan, if a bill should reach his desk. Governor Brown's interest had not become support, and on February 10, 1966, his Director of Finance, Hale Champion, went on record in favor of state service centers as a preferable alternative to the Ombudsman. Governor Reagan has not taken a final stand. At a meeting between Speaker Unruh and Governor-elect Reagan on December 18, 1966, Reagan had "no comment" on Unruh's request for support on this issue.

The Politics of Adoption

The process of legitimization in California can be seen quite clearly. Respectability has been lent to the Ombudsman idea by the New Zealand and Swedish Ombudsmen, the Israeli State Comptroller, several research institutes, various foundations and public service organizations, and a number of civil rights lobbies. The Unruh Bill has been heard by legislative committees on nine occasions, ranging from a few minutes to a full day each. The press has given adequate coverage to these events, and to comparable activities at local and Federal levels, and has responded with editorials which have been more often "thumbs-up" than "thumbs-down."

PUBLIC OPINION

Still, publicity has not attained the regularity and repetitiveness which is necessary for the penetration of popular consciousness. On a question-and-answer radio program in the San Francisco area during the spring of 1967, for example, the Ombudsman question stimulated only a single response, and the moderator had to drop the topic and to return to Viet Nam and taxes. Talk of Ombudsman has spread beyond elite legitimizing groups only when tied to the controversial issue of civilian police review boards, as in New York City, and, to a lesser extent, Oakland, California. The office is not likely to be swept into being by grassroots clamor.

It is unlikely that an election will ever turn on the Ombudsman issue. In two instances to date, its use as the crux of a campaign has proven to be not harmful and probably helpful to the candidates who adopted it. With Ombudsman lapel buttons, bumper stickers and

[7] Letter dated August 10, 1967.

letter openers for the November, 1966, State Senate race in Connecticut, Republican Lawrence DeNardis lost the election, but ran ahead of the Republican ticket in his district. Democratic State Senator Edmundo R. Delgado won office, and his subsequent bill, S.B. 10/1967, came within a single vote of passing the New Mexico Senate. Indeed, an apparent tie was first broken in favor of the Ombudsman measure by Republican Lt. Governor E. Lee Francis. Fifteen minutes later, a tabulation error was announced, and the proposal was declared to be defeated 20 to 21.

The upshot, then, is that public opinion is inchoate and permissive. It will probably be left to Ombudsmen themselves to make the institution part of American folklore. Meanwhile, the forum for legitimizing the concept of Ombudsman remains in the pertinent legislative bodies. Here, the method is basically Socratic, with dialogue among legislators, lobbyists, and representatives of executive agencies.

GIVE AND TAKE

As a result of testimony from tax officials at the 1965 hearings of the Assembly Committee on Government Organization, for example, the 1967 bill was amended to prohibit the Ombudsman from unilateral disclosure of information gotten by him from tax returns. In 1967, the proposal was amended several times to meet specific objections. Thus, the exclusion of local government, the Legislature, the judiciary and the State bar was made explicit. Changes such as these silence opposition and sometimes win new support. In the case of the district attorneys' and peace officers' lobbies, however, not even the express exclusion of any "county, city, whether general law or chartered, city and county, town, school district, municipal corporation, district, political subdivision, or other local public agency" could convince them that a State Ombudsman was not a camel's nose in the tent of local law enforcement, possibly leading to the creation of civilian police review boards or their equivalent.

PROBLEM OF SIZE

Some objections have been counsels of despair, such as that the job is too big to be done. This is usually a reference to the factor of population, most obvious at the Federal level. Faced with a populace twenty times that of California, Messrs. Reuss and Long have each adopted half of the British sop to size. Congressman Reuss would filter complaints to the Administrative Counsel through members of Congress, and Senator Long would limit the jurisdiction of the Administrative Ombudsman to the Bureau of Prisons, Internal Revenue Service, Social Security Administration and Veterans Administration. Neither of these compromises is crippling. The short Long list could later be lengthened, and there is nothing in the Reuss bill (or in the British Act) requiring the complainant to go through the legislator of his own district.

Another potential Federal Ombudsman is the Chairman of the Administrative Conference of the United States. The Conference was authorized by Public Law 88-499 in 1964, and the Chairman is empowered "to make inquiries into matters he deems important . . .", including matters proposed by persons inside or outside the Federal Government." As yet, the President has not filled the position.

Other solutions to the challenge of numbers have been presented in earlier chapters. The Ombudsman could be collegial, as it is in fact in Sweden, where the Deputy JO acts entirely on his own as to cases which he undertakes. Division of labor could as well be functional—with a social welfare Ombudsman, an incarceration Ombudsman, etc.—or geographic, the latter being the thoughtful recommendation made in Chapter 4. Finally, one might consider the alternative of a bureaucratic Ombudsman, as suggested in Chapter 2. The success of the Israeli State Comptroller in carrying out an Ombudsman function suggests that legislative auditors are possible American repositories for Ombudsmanic responsibility—if the office chief is willing and able to see his job as more than mere bookkeeping.

Finally, one might easily contemplate a plurality of Ombudsmen—for example, the Reuss proposal plus the Long proposal plus the United States Comptroller-General and the Chairman of the Administrative Conference. To avoid duplication of effort, one office should not entertain a complaint which is under consideration by another. This is precisely the rule followed by JO and JK in Finland and Sweden, and it is prescribed in the New York State Dunne-Jones bill cited in the preceding chapter. In California, the only concession made to size has been to limit the jurisdiction of the proposed Ombudsman strictly to State administrative agencies.

IMPARTIALITY

Another counsel of despair has been that one could never find the man who could do the job, and that the office would inevitably become partisan in its operation, either attacking or apologizing for administration. The search for Ombudsmen is part of the broader search for impartial expertise. We seek it in our judges, in our administrators, and, indeed, in our legislators—the last by a kind of reciprocal adjudication in which a shifting and hopefully disinterested majority passes upon the proposals of the committed few. As intimated in Chapter 3, legislators are sometimes advocates and sometimes judges, among other roles which they may assume. Put in this context, then, it is fair to say that the Diogenes argument proves too much:

if an impartial Ombudsman is inconceivable, then all is spoils—judges are servile, legislators are pawns, administrators are hacks. In the present writer's opinion, this, happily, is not the case.

The reason that one can have impartial public servants at all is that the means of appointment is subordinate in impact to the conditions of service. Federal judges are appointed by the President and confirmed by the United States Senate, a highly political process. Yet, life tenure frees them from servility. In many states, judgeships are effectively, if not formally, tenured, with comparable consequences. Merit civil service systems underpin impartiality in American local, state and Federal government administration. The Ombudsman has been traditionally an arm of the legislature—but an independent arm. And the job he performs is quasi-judicial. As indicated in Chapter 2, there is no reason why we cannot match the men who have already been found to serve as Ombudsmen; these have been emphatically impartial. Tenure, adequate salary and the shared expectations for his office go far to assure impartiality, no matter how the Ombudsman is appointed. These expectations should lead to his being chosen by general accord, regardless of the formal mechanisms which must be followed.

POLICE REVIEW

At the local level—and, as already indicated, with some spillover at the state level—the most common argument against Ombudsman has been that it is a substitute civilian police review board. The major premise of this argument is that the police should be accountable to no one. Another form of the absolute sanctity position is that secrecy is essential for efficiency. But review, by definition, is after the fact. The awareness of the possibility of review ought to make policemen more circumspect, and the consequence of review may be to improve police effectiveness. Such is the import of the Swedish and New Zealand cases on police supervision which are supplied in Chapter 1, two of which involve improper commitment or interrogation, while the other two document cases of inept and even lackadaisical law enforcement.
. .It is true that the first line of supervision should be within the police department—as it should be for any executive agency, each of which has primary responsibility for keeping its own house clean. One may also appreciate the distaste which policemen have for being singled out for special scrutiny. The Ombudsman office meets both of these objections. It subjects the police to the same surveillance as other agencies, and subjects all agencies to second-line supervision, as a backstop to internal control.

LEGISLATIVE OMBUDSMEN

The most frequent and emphatic objection to Ombudsman has been that elected representatives—Congressmen, state legislators, county supervisors and city councilors—are already doing the job. If they are not, it is argued, they ought to be. And, in any event, no one else should be allowed to do it. As already noted, this argument has inspired the Institute of Governmental Studies and the Institute for Local Self Government to study the adequacy of present complaint mechanisms, including the intervention of elected officials. And Chapter 3 is focused explicitly upon the lawmaker's role as Ombudsman.

No matter how good a job some legislators may be doing, all are not doing equally well. This disparity alone should compel the establishment of a parallel office, for the benefit of those whose elected representatives are relatively aloof, feeble or incompetent. The Ombudsman should be able to match the expertise of the most perspicacious lawmaker in treating with the bureaucracy.

Even the able and energetic legislator lacks another crucial quality of an Ombudsman. Besides expertise, the Ombudsman has impartiality. As a partisan politician, the elected official lacks this quality, or at least he may seem to lack it. The lawmaker, then, is suspected of bias in his judgment as to the validity of a constituent complaint. He may attack or defend the administration, uphold or reject the grievance, it is feared, upon calculations of advantage which are extraneous to the merits of the complaint. His potential for the reasoned persuasion of an administrator is correspondingly undercut. And the suspicion arises that he may be subjecting the administrator to pressure other than sweet reason, by asking for special favor beyond or even in violation of the law.

While it is a legitimate objection to the lawmaker as Ombudsman that his judgment may be impure, the more frequent occurrence is that the legislator simply makes no judgment at all. He receives a complaint which he has neither the time nor the ability to evaluate, and passes the complaint on to the agency which has been accused. Ironically, others may interpret this abdication of judgment as an expression of judgment. It was the appreciation of this dilemma for the lawmaker which first led Speaker Unruh to espouse the Ombudsman idea.

CONSEQUENCES OF INCUMBENCY

Some legislators argue that an Ombudsman would at best only duplicate what the lawmaker is already doing because of self-interest arising out of the calculation of case work as a significant aid to re-election. By helping a constituent, one may be paying for past or currying future favor. When the potential benefit is multiplied to take

family and friends into account, one can understand that ballot-conscious officials are anxious to perform this kind of service.

A related fear is that the Ombudsman may use his position as a springboard to popular election. In the California bill, the Ombudsman is not "eligible for election to the Legislature nor to any state-wide office for a period of two years after leaving the office of Ombudsman." Little can be found to justify such a provision, other than the mollification of nervous office holders.

These phenomena are part of the politics of incumbency. Though divided by party, chamber and branch, incumbents share one common interest: they are all in office, and they would like to stay there. The gerrymander is a classic situation for the operation of the security principle; a minority party incumbent will find it difficult to vote against a bill for redistricting which gives him a safe seat, even though that safety may cost his party a seat in the neighboring district. Rules governing elections, the very designation of "Incumbent" on the ballot, are all shaped by those who have a vivid awareness of potential personal consequences.

No thorough study has been made, and the politician's hunch is as good as the social scientist's as to the vote value of case work. One cannot blame the voteseeker for leaving no stone unturned. As far as the Ombudsman is concerned, however, two considerations ameliorate the inroads which he might make on the officeholder's constituent services.

First, requests for intervention for the relief of specific grievances against the bureaucracy are but a fraction of the total demands made by voters upon their chosen representatives. Other demands include acting as a travel agency for visitors from the home district, seeking and sometimes finding or providing employment, supplying information of all sorts, including that requested by students for their homework, and intervening with governmental or private agencies to ask for special favor, etc. None of these, including the last, would fall within the Ombudsman's proper ambit. Second, people may continue to take complaints suitable for the Ombudsman to their elected legislators. The latter are equally free to refer these grievances to the Ombudsman. As already noted, Congressman Reuss's approach would require complaints to be transmitted to the Ombudsman by a member of Congress. Free enterprise is preferable, as a wholesome competition in the servicing of complaints would stimulate both lawmaker and Ombudsman to renewed diligence.

BLAND SCEPTICISM

Most of the voices against Ombudsman proposals have *not* been motivated by a clear conviction of the validity of the objections just enumerated. Rather, the legislators have simply remained unconvinced of the need for or efficacy of an Ombudsman. Even though modest, the office does cost money, and, it is argued, once established, it is difficult to dismantle. Had it been asked of him in the Senate, Speaker Unruh was willing to provide in his bill that the office of Ombudsman would lapse unless affirmatively renewed at a later session of the California Legislature.

What is most likely to convince these bland sceptics is the successful operation of an Ombudsman office in other American jurisdictions. Once convinced, most lawmakers will not let considerations of possible personal advantage from case work interfere with their judgment. While a particular proposal at a given time and place may have a slender chance of adoption, some of the many proposals are bound to break through, as the Hawaiian experience indicates. With initial success, the burden of proof will shift to the opponents of Ombudsman, and a wave of enactments may well ensue.

The California Commission On Judicial Qualifications

Meanwhile, in the absence of example, we are forced to rely upon analogy with foreign Ombudsmen and partial Ombudsmen, such as the Nassau Public Protector, and upon simulation, as with the Buffalo experiment of the Citizens Administrative Service, described in Chapter 4. Being few, such analogies and trials are precious. There is another, then, which we cannot afford to ignore. It is a judicial Ombudsman, the California Commission on Judicial Qualifications. Its origins were, briefly, as follows: [8]

> [Former] Chief Justice [Phil S.] Gibson pressed for a state constitutional amendment that would give the California Supreme Court full power to remove unfit judges at every level, including its own. The state legislature and California voters overwhelmingly approved such an amendment in 1960. The bench-dominated body that has been set up to do the high court's investigating work is a nine-member . . . commission [which] operates out of San Francisco under Executive Secretary Jack E. Frankel, an able, tactful lawyer . . .

As amended in 1966, Article VI of the California State Constitution provides (Section 18 (c)) that:

> On recommendation of the Commission on Judicial Qualifications the Supreme Court may (1) retire a judge for disability that seriously interferes with the performance of his duties and is or is likely to become permanent, and (2) censure or remove a judge for action . . . that constitutes wilful misconduct in office, wilful and persistent failure to perform his duties,

[8] *Time Magazine*, March 26, 1965, p. 63.

habitual intemperance, or conduct prejudicial to the administration of justice that brings the judicial office into disrepute.

On only a single occasion, in 1964, has the Commission recommended the removal of a judge to the Supreme Court. The Court did not comply. Yet, from one-half to one percent of California's approximately one thousand judges have retired or resigned each year rather than face further Commission investigation and possible recommendation for removal. As the proceedings are confidential, it is not exposure which these judges fear. Nor are they threatened, normally, with loss of pension. Instead, they have a sober realization of the validity of the charges against them—usually mental or physical disability.

OMBUDSMAN FUNCTION

The cumulative impact of an annual handful of resignations is substantial in helping to maintain a vigorous and able judiciary. But this is not the only and perhaps not the most important activity of the Commission on Judicial Qualifications. As stated in the 1963 Report of the Commission (pp. 2-3):

1. It is useful for the public to have a place to register alleged grievances against judges even though seldom is there a basis for further Commission action from such a complaint. An official state body to receive complaints against judicial officers furnishes as much protection to honest and dedicated judges as to the public.
2. Indirectly, the Commission's very existence as a standing tribunal empowered to investigate and act has effected standards of conduct and ethics . . . [T]his is intangible and difficult to assess . . .
3. Some of the Commission's inquiries during the year, while revealing questionable practices, were deemed not to justify a removal proceeding. Sometimes transmitting reports of such shortcomings to the judge for his reply has had a beneficial effect . . .

The techniques used to investigate these complaints are very much like those followed by Ombudsmen in probing complaints against administration. For example, the Commission has subpoena power, but it is very seldom used. According to the Commission's 1964 Report (p. 1):

The Commission's procedure is to close complaints which are clearly unfounded; to evaluate and, if warranted, make inquiry and check on apparently actionable allegations; then, [when] appropriate, to contact the judge by letter or in person and, in the event it is justified, hold a preliminary investigation . . . [which] may also be accompanied by a field investigation.

In the calendar year 1966, nine judges resigned or retired during the course of Commission investigation into their continued capacity to perform as judges. Perhaps a few of these might have stepped down anyway. A summary of the Commission's activity during that year is given in the 1966 Report to the Governor (p. 3) :

> During 1966, of 75 complaints registered against judges, 33 required some investigation or inquiry. On 29 occasions, including the nine terminations, there was correspondence or personal interview with the judge . . . In a few instances, after considering the judge's answer and completing its investigation, the Commission concluded there were derelictions and shortcomings that did not warrant removal proceedings but did justify criticism, and for which the judge was admonished by the Commission.
>
> In recent years such infractions have included neglect and inattention to duties, disregard for rules and standards of practice, arrogance and aggravated discourtesy, and violations of canons of judicial ethics. Usually specific changes or improvements have resulted from the action of the Commission.

The comparable figures for 1965 were: 85 complaints alleging specific charges against a judge; 38 inquiries; 29 judges contacted; eight personal interviews with judges; six full investigations preliminary to recommendation of removal; and, four resignations. During the same year, the Swedish JO received 134 complaints against judges (excluding administrative court judges), and took up another 97 on his own initiative, for a total of 231.

COMPARISONS TO SWEDEN

Comparisons to the Swedish Ombudsman are striking. First, the original thrust of the JO was to the courts. Second, the Swedish official has power to prosecute, but now uses it rarely and instead issues "reminders." Likewise, the authority of the Commission on Judicial Qualifications is directed to the judiciary. And, it has the power to prosecute removals before the Supreme Court, but has used this power only once, and has instead relied upon censure.

The main difference in mode of operation is that Swedish inquiries and wrist-slappings are publicized, while those in California are not. As noted in Chapter 1, Sweden has a general principle of openness of governmental activity, including that of the JO. The greater number of cases taken up by the latter may be attributed to the broader range of accusations which he will investigate. He may, for example, second-guess the judges on the law, if he believes their interpretation to be faulty. In California and elsewhere, review of the reasoning of a case is left to the appellate courts.

The California Commission on Judicial Qualifications, then, represents the independent invention of a control device instituted in Sweden 150 to 200 years ago. Like the Norwegian Military Ombudsman institution, the California office is collegial, acting in practice through a single official, here the Executive Secretary. The Commission meets the three crucial tests of Ombudsmanhood: impartiality, expertise, and reliance upon reasoned persuasion. Impartiality flows from independence. The Commissioners have four-year terms. Five judges are appointed by the Supreme Court from three lower tiers of courts; the State Bar appoints two lawyers; and, the Governor appoints two laymen.

Ironically, the first implementation of Ombudsman in California has come at the most sensitive level of government, that of the judiciary. States with a Commission on Judicial Qualifications, or its equivalent, may easily exclude the courts from the supervision of a general Ombudsman. There is nearly universal agreement that the Commission has been a success. Its emulation has been recommended by the President's Crime Commission and the American Judicature Society. Adoption is being considered in a number of states, and comparable commissions have already been established in Colorado, Florida, Maryland, Nebraska, and Texas.

Courts have primary responsibility, individual and collective, for their own supervision. The Commission on Judicial Qualifications is a control on self-control. It demonstrates that a judges' "Civilian Review Board" will work to resolve complaints and to improve efficiency, without impairing independence.

Conclusion

Among the Ombudsman's worst enemies are some of his best friends: those who expect too much of him. The Ombudsman can encourage continuing improvement in a basically sound and honest administration. He cannot correct basic injustices, even though he may protest against them. Problems of poverty, prejudice and ignorance will not be solved by shunting them to the shoulders of a single Don Quixote. The more modest but still important contributions which one might expect from an Ombudsman will be frustrated if he is charged to change the very climate of our society, to cool the long hot summer.

Ombudsmania can be identified by one key characteristic: it would give the Ombudsman power—power to change administrative decisions, power to prosecute brutal policemen, power to modify faulty regulations. Such a Superombudsman would be a chief executive, legislature and judge rolled into one. The frustrations of trial-and-error democracy sometimes give rise to an understandable longing for an all-powerful father-figure. By virtue of his wisdom, an Ombudsman would seem to fill the role; this same wisdom leads him to decline it. He declines not only because such a role would be authoritarian, but because he cannot in fact fill it. For him to try to do so would be merely to create a paragovernment recapitulating all the shortcomings of the primary government, and then some. Immediately, the new leader would become enamored of his own decisions, and we would be seeking still another unwatched watcher.

Painful and slow though they may sometimes be, the basic institutions and processes of American government are not radically altered by the addition of Ombudsmen. What, then, does an Ombudsman accomplish that present institutions do not? Any particular grievance could conceivably be rectified through the intervention of a friend, neighbor, relative, lawyer, newspaper, or legislator—or even directly by the agency which inflicted it. For the equal protection of the laws, however, there should be someone to whom anyone may turn—and there are people with neither friends, relatives, or neighbors, etc. Moreover, someone should be able to take up cases not handled by stump lawyers, the press, and lawmakers. At the level of resolution of individual complaints, then, the Ombudsman is a fail-safe device, whose need is demonstrated by the frequency of its use.

The lawyer's fee often makes him inaccessible. When others help, they do so as a charity. Substitution of an Ombudsman means that evil imposed by government is rectified by government, and rectified as a primary responsibility rather than as a haphazard favor from a busy legislator. Lawmakers have a right to intervene, and so do we all; the Ombudsman has a duty to do so, in cases which he believes merit it. Others who volunteer usually lack expertise and impartiality; they are amateurs and advocates. Each of these characteristics makes them less effective. Partly, then, what the Ombudsman adds is simply that he does the job bigger and better.

The unique contribution of the Ombudsman stands out more clearly in the zone of secondary impact. Citizens' complaints are symptoms of governmental malaise. To be useful in diagnosis, they must be examined by a specialist. Presently, if seen by anyone, they are viewed by practitioners who seek mere symptomatic relief. While accomplishing the latter, the Ombudsman adds prevention. He does not root out underlying causes of societal sickness. While dispensing quinine to dampen the fevers of malaria, the Ombudsman also swats a few mosquitos. But it is still up to the legislature to drain the swamps. Seen in this perspective, the result remains that the Ombudsman makes a significant contribution to the improvement of administration.

Finally at a third level, the Ombudsman assists in the restoration of balance between the legislative and executive branches of our government. Size and complexity have overwhelmed often underpaid, understaffed and over-extended lawmakers. The executive branch, and the military-industrial complex of which President Dwight Eisenhower warned us to be watchful, have the men, money and mental muscle. The Ombudsman can free the legislator from the harassment of trivia, while turning minute complaints into a mosaic which the legislature should find helpful in supervising bureaucracy. No other complaint-handling mechanism has this potential.

Being careful to prevent overextension of the Ombudsman does not mean that one cannot be imaginative in adapting the office to the American scene. In Massachusetts, for example, the proposal of Secretary of the Commonwealth Kevin H. White and State Representative James R. Nolen would wed the Ombudsman job to two related functions. In House Bill 2677/1967, to establish "the Massachusetts Information and Referral Agency of the Office of Ombudsman," (comparable to the 1966 measure sponsored also by Representative Chandler H. Stevens) the Ombudsman is directed to "keep a record of the existence and procedures of all boards of appeal and similar agencies," which is to "be made available to all interested persons upon request . . ." Here, the Ombudsman would provide legal aid in the administrative sphere, where it has been sorely lacking. Those dealing with the bureaucracy would come to the Ombudsman for advice while action is pending, and not merely after the fact with a grievance.

Secondly, H.B. 2677 would also charge the Ombudsman to "keep a record of all public publications of the commonwealth; provide detailed information on the purposes, scope and procedures of all major programs . . ." This duty might easily be construed as a mandate to serve as an overseer and coordinator on questions of administrative procedure as a kind of continuing "Little Hoover" commission.

Each of these services represents a substantial increment to the traditional complaint-handling function of Ombudsman. The Massachusetts office would probably require a three-fold division, with adequate staff for each. As phrased in the bill, the legal aid function stops short of advocacy, so that the Ombudsman would not be the attorney in a case upon which he might later have to pass as judge. (An administrative public defender should be kept outside the Ombudsman's office.) The additional tasks in the White-Nolen bill would add to the Ombudsman's expertise, without impairing his impartiality or altering his exclusive reliance on reasoned persuasion. It would broaden his service function at the consumer end of government and systematize his contribution to the improvement of administration.

City, county, state or nation; single, plural, collegial or bureaucratic; filtered and limited or direct and general: there comes an existential moment when deliberation must give way to judgment and action. Those who would act on Ombudsman might well turn to Professor

Walter Gellhorn's statute in the appendix which follows, for a model. The institution is quite flexible, however, and—as Professor Gellhorn himself has noted—there is no particular virtue in making it uniform. The experience of a variety of Ombudsmen would be instructive. *Fiat Ombudsman!*

Walter Gellhorn

Appendix:
Annotated Model Ombudsman Statute

What follows is a "model" bill to establish the ombudsman system in American states and cities. The bill can be adapted to the needs of various states with little change. It is also suitable as a local enactment by a municipality that has constitutional or statutory authority to create its own governmental instrumentalities. The extent of allowable home rule must, of course, be considered closely by local counsel.

This draft builds upon foundations others have laid. Ralph Nader drafted the first ombudsman bill for consideration by an American legislature; it was introduced in Connecticut in 1963. The first model bill was creditably prepared by the Harvard Student Legislative Re-

WALTER GELLHORN, *one of the nation's leading authorities on the Ombudsman, is Betts Professor of Law at Columbia University. He has had extensive experience in public administration, having served the Justice and Interior Departments, the Social Security Administration, the Office of Price Administration, and the War Labor Board, among others. Professor Gellhorn has written numerous volumes on law and administration, the most recent being* When Americans Complain, *a study of governmental grievance procedures, and* Ombudsmen and Others, *a work on citizens' protectors in nine countries.*

search Bureau.[1] Both of the proposals leaned heavily on the New
Zealand ombudsman statute of 1962, which itself had been influenced
by the Danish law. Other American proposals have also been helpful,
notably Senator Edward V. Long's bill to establish a District of Columbia ombudsman and the bill of Senator Jack E. Bronston and Assemblyman S. William Green to create an office of public redress in the State
of New York.

A BILL

To establish the Office of Ombudsman

in ....

[Enactment clause in locally appropriate form]

Section 1. *Short title.* This Act may be cited as The.................
[insert name of state, city, or other entity] Ombudsman Act.

COMMENT. The "foreign-sounding word" *ombudsman* has gained
wide usage in America and many other countries. Its distinctiveness
makes it preferable to more usual official titles such as "commissioner" or "director." The position, new in American experience,
deserves a new identification.

Section 2. *Definitions.* As used in this Act, the term

(a) "Administrative agency" means any department or other governmental unit, any official, or any employee of ....
[state, city, or other entity involved] acting or purporting to act by
reason of connection with .... [again insert name of
state, city, or other entity]; but it does not include (1) any court or
judge or appurtenant judicial staff, (2) the members, committees, or
staffs of the .... [insert name of the legislative body,
e.g., City Council] or (3) the .... [insert title of chief
executive] or his personal staff.

COMMENT. Traditional immunization of courts against extra-judicial
scrutiny argues against permitting an American ombudsman to
inquire into a judge's behavior. Legislators and the chief executive
are directly answerable to the electorate; their conduct in office
tends in any event to be conspicuous and subject to continuous
political examination. Other elected officials (such as, in some jurisdictions, members of regulatory bodies, law enforcement officials,
and educational administrators) are less immediately involved in
policy making and are engaged chiefly in administrative matters
indistinguishable from those performed by non-elected officials generally. Their inclusion within the reach of the Ombudsman Act
therefore seems desirable.

---

[1] "A State Statute to Create the Office of Ombudsman," *Harvard Journal of Legis-
lation,* 2 (June, 1965), 213-38, reprinted as an appendix to the March 7, 1966,
Hearing on Ombudsman of the United States Senate Judiciary Subcommittee on
Administrative Practice and Procedure, at pp. 336-61.

If a state bill were to be drafted, a fourth exception should be considered, as follows: " (4) any instrumentality of any political subdivision of the state." This would make clear that the state ombudsman should avoid dealing with municipal and county affairs, if state superintendence of local officialdom is deemed undesirable. In a state-wide bill prudence may also dictate a fifth specific exclusion to make indisputable that interstate bodies such as the Port of New York Authority or the Delaware River water resources board are not meant to be reached, though this specificity is perhaps not really needed: " (5) any instrumentality formed pursuant to an interstate compact and answerable to more than one state."

(b) "Administrative act" includes every action (such as decisions, omissions, recommendations, practices, or procedures) of an administrative agency.

Section 3. *Establishment of office.* The office of Ombudsman is hereby established as an independent agency of .... [insert name of state, city, or other entity]

COMMENT. Whether the Ombudsman can be a wholly independent entity or must instead be included within the Executive or the Legislative Branch depends upon the local constitution or charter. Organizational detachment is the desired estate if it can be achieved constitutionally.

Section 4. *Appointment.* The .... [insert title of chief executive] shall appoint the Ombudsman, subject to confirmation by two-thirds of the members of each chamber of the .... [insert name of legislative body] present and voting.

COMMENT. In foreign countries the ombudsman has been elected by the legislature. The governmental structure in those countries differs, however, from the American pattern. Appointive officials, whatever their nature, are customarily chosen in American jurisdictions by the Chief Executive, subject sometimes to legislative confirmation. The present proposal contemplates confirmation by an unusually substantial vote in both chambers (if two exist) rather than in the Senate alone. This is intended to stress the "non-political" nature of the appointment and to reflect the need for general acceptability of the person chosen. Whether the required majority be two-thirds of those voting or some other figure can, of course, be fixed in accord with local preference or precedent.

Some persons favor direct legislative selection, without participation by the Executive. Thus, a Florida bill proposes simply that the ombudsman is to be "appointed by agreement of the president of senate and the speaker of the house subject to confirmation by a majority of the members of each chamber of the legislature." A

Connecticut bill provides that one or more candidates "shall be selected by the judiciary committee and reported to the general assembly," after which the ombudsman is to be "elected by a vote of either a majority of each major political party or a two-thirds majority of the general assembly." A more elaborate plan has been advanced in California. It envisages a "Joint Legislative Committee on Administrative Justice" composed of three members of each house from both political parties. From a list prepared by a blue ribbon commission, the committee is to nominate the ombudsman by an absolute majority vote, and the nominee is to be "appointed to the office of Ombudsman by concurrent resolution of the Legislature."

All the plans emphasize the desirability of "de-politicalizing" the selection process.

The California plan contemplates that the joint committee will have a continuing existence and will be available for consultation by the ombudsman "as he deems necessary to the execution of his powers and duties." No matter how the office of Ombudsman may be filled, some such provision in the legislature's own internal organization would be desirable so that the ombudsman can have a regular point of contact when needed.

Section 5. *Qualifications.* The Ombudsman shall be a person well equipped to analyze problems of law, administration, and public policy, and shall not be actively involved in partisan affairs.

COMMENT. Efforts to define the qualities sought in an ombudsman tend to result in a catalogue of human virtues, leading one person to remark that if ever such a man were found, he would instantly be cast in bronze rather than appointed to a mundane office. Experience abroad points clearly to the desirability of the ombudsman's having a legal background because he must deal with many grievances that hinge on analysis of statutes and rulings. Requiring any specific experience or absolutely excluding any category of persons (for example, those who have recently been legislators or have held other office) seems undesirable. The consensus of opinion that will presumably support legislative confirmation should be an adequate barrier against unsuitable nominees.

Section 6. *Term of office.* (a) The Ombudsman shall serve for a term of five years, unless removed by vote of two-thirds of the members of each of the two chambers of the .... [insert name of legislative body] upon their determining that he has become incapacitated or has been guilty of neglect of duty or misconduct;

COMMENT. The Ombudsman should be secure, but not absolutely untouchable. The proposed provision would adequately guard against casual threats. An alternative would be to provide simply that the Ombudsman shall serve out his term, unless "impeached by the [legislature] in accord with the procedures prescribed by the constitution." The likelihood of removal is extremely slim, in any event.

(b) If the office of Ombudsman becomes vacant for any cause, the Deputy Ombudsman shall serve as Acting Ombudsman until an Ombudsman has been appointed for a full term.

COMMENT. Whether the term of office should be more or less than five years is not demonstrable. Abroad, no term exceeds four years. Here, some persons believe that the detachment of the Ombudsman from the Chief Executive will be accentuated if a vacancy does not automatically coincide with the inauguration of a new mayor or governor. Some advocate an even longer term than five years. The length of the term is not very important. If the institution proves its worth, tinkering with the Ombudsman's independence would be so politically perilous as to be altogether unlikely. To guard against sudden attacks upon an incumbent, removability should be made difficult, as has been done in this draft. As for vacancies, a stopgap until a permanent appointment can be made for a full term is preferable to an appointment merely for the balance of the unexpired term, as others have sometimes suggested.

In New Zealand the incumbent Ombudsman continues serving beyond the expiration of his term, unless and until a successor has qualified. Although this assures continuity of Ombudsman services, it means that the hold-over Ombudsman has no security of tenure, a circumstance that may at least theoretically expose him to undesirable pressures.

Section 7. *Salary*. The Ombudsman shall receive the same salary, allowances, and related benefits as the chief judge of the highest court of . . . . [name of state]

COMMENT. Setting the Ombudsman's pay and perquisites at the level of the highest ranking judge will give the new office a desirably high prestige, will eliminate wrangling now and in the future about the appropriate dollar amount of the Ombudsman's salary, and will avoid the obsolescence that would soon occur if the desired salary were to be precisely stated. If the Ombudsman is connected with a governmental subdivision rather than with the state itself, some other comparison would be appropriate.

Section 8. *Organization of office*. (a) The Ombudsman may select, appoint, and compensate as he may see fit (within the amount available by appropriation) such assistants and employees as he may deem necessary to discharge his responsibilities under this Act;

(b) The Ombudsman shall designate one of his assistants to be the Deputy Ombudsman, with authority to act in his stead when he himself is disabled or protractedly absent;

(c) The Ombudsman may delegate to other members of his staff any of his authority or duties under this Act except this power of delegation and the duty of formally making recommendations to administrative agencies or reports to the .... [insert title of chief executive] or the .... [insert name of legislative body].

COMMENT. This section gives the Ombudsman a free hand in staffing his office, without even the restraints of civil service and classification acts. The highly personal nature of the Ombudsman's work, coupled with its essentially experimental nature, justifies giving this leeway to so highly placed and, by hypothesis, responsible an official. For the same reasons the Ombudsman has been given a free choice about assigning duties and subdelegating powers, with the single limitation that when criticisms or proposals for change are to be voiced in a formal manner, only the Ombudsman himself may be heard (except when the Deputy Ombudsman is in full charge during the Ombudsman's disability or protracted absence) .

Section 9. *Powers.* The Ombudsman shall have the following powers:

(a) He may investigate, on complaint or on his own motion, any administrative act of any administrative agency;

COMMENT. The power to investigate should be stated unqualifiedly, though later sections will indicate the grounds that justify action by him and will thus suggest the occasions on which investigation would be suitable. Experience abroad shows that efforts to define jurisdiction have caused much laborious and essentially unproductive hairsplitting; a more general grant of power to investigate will eliminate some "legalistic" analysis in the beginning of the Ombudsman's work, but his own discretion will lead him to set sensible boundaries to the areas within which he will investigate, lest he be crushed by the burden of unproductive work.

(b) He may prescribe the methods by which complaints are to be made, received, and acted upon; he may determine the scope and manner of investigations to be made; and, subject to the requirements of this Act, he may determine the form, frequency, and distribution of his conclusions and recommendations;

COMMENT. Some foreign statutes require that complaints be written. Leaving matters of this kind to the Ombudsman's choice in the light of experience is preferable. Similarly, giving the Ombudsman power to shape his own investigations is desirable; any implication that he should utilize the same method at all times should be avoided, as should any requirement of formal hearing of an adversary nature. If a proceeding for the taking of testimony were in fact to occur, it should be perceived as an element of an investigation rather than as a proceeding in the nature of a trial. Hence its content need not necessarily be the same as would normally be demanded in a formal adjudicatory hearing.

(c) He may request and shall be given by each administrative agency the assistance and information he deems necessary for the discharge of his responsibilities; he may examine the records and documents of all administrative agencies; and he may enter and inspect premises within any administrative agency's control.

COMMENT. Experience elsewhere suggests that the Ombudsman will be given ready access to official papers or other information within the administrative agency. Cooperative working relationships have been readily established so that the Ombudsman's need for documentary material has not conflicted with the administrators' continuing need to use the same material. As for inspection of administrative offices and installations, this draft gives the Ombudsman power to inspect but imposes no duty to do so routinely, as has been required of the Ombudsmen in several Scandinavian countries.

(d) He may issue a subpoena to compel any person to appear, give sworn testimony, or produce documentary or other evidence the Ombudsman deems relevant to a matter under his inquiry.

COMMENT. Every existing Ombudsman statute provides very broadly for the use of compulsory process in order to obtain needed information. In point of fact, however, the subpoena power has virtually never been used abroad, since information has been freely given. Concern has nevertheless been expressed in this country that wide-ranging inquiries into public administration might lead to burdensome demands. Hence Section 18, below, takes pains to stress protections for witnesses, even though the occasions for bringing them into play are likely to be very few indeed.

(e) He may undertake, participate in, or cooperate with general studies or inquiries, whether or not related to any particular administrative agency or any particular administrative act, if he believes that they may enhance knowledge about or lead to improvements in the functioning of administrative agencies.

COMMENT. If foreign experience is an accurate guide, work on individual complaints will chiefly preoccupy the Ombudsman's energies and attention. Nonetheless, he should be clearly empowered to address himself to general problems (some of which, indeed, may not be reflected at all in current complaints) and should be free to work not only with other governmental bodies, but also with non-governmental research enterprises which, in the United States much more than in most other countries, provide a great deal of the manpower, insight, and enthusiasm that underlie governmental improvements.

Section 10. *Matters appropriate for investigation.* (a) In selecting matters for his attention, the Ombudsman should address himself particularly to an administrative act that might be

1. contrary to law or regulation;
2. unreasonable, unfair, oppressive, or inconsistent with the general course of an administrative agency's functioning;
3. mistaken in law or arbitrary in ascertainments of fact;
4. improper in motivation or based on irrelevant considerations;
5. unclear or inadequately explained when reasons should have been revealed;
6. inefficiently performed; or
7. otherwise objectionable;

COMMENT. The statute desirably details the kinds of administrative acts whose occurrence has chiefly generated demands for the Ombudsman system. This draft sets them forth as guides, not as limitations. The Ombudsman is told to devote himself to these types of problems, but he need not feel himself confined to them if the catalog later be found to be incomplete. Subsection (3) refers to acts that rest on arbitrary ascertainments of fact. Very clearly, the Ombudsman must not attempt to be a super-administrator, doing over again what specialized administrators have already done and, if he disagrees, substituting his judgment for theirs. In some instances, however, the propriety of an administrative act may rest wholly on a factual determination that in turn rests on an excessively flimsy foundation. As in cases that go to courts for review, the Ombudsman should not regard as "arbitrary" anything and everything with which he disagrees; but he should be in a position to say, in essence, that reasonable men would not have found the facts in the way the administrator did.

Subsection (5) is not intended to create a new legal requirement that findings of fact and conclusions of law accompany every administrative act. It means merely that official actions should be understandable and, usually, should be explained when those affected by them seek fuller understanding. Experience abroad shows that this is one of the areas most fruitfully cultivated by Ombudsmen.

Subsection (6) refers to administrative acts that may lie within the zone of legality, but might nevertheless be subject to improvement in the future. Thus, for example, the form of decision given by a Scandinavian administrator to old age pensioners caused later distress because the pensioners read into it some hopes that were not justified by existing law. The Ombudsman found nothing improper in the decisions that had been made, but suggested some purely stylistic changes that eliminated the bewildering "officialese" previously in use.

Subsection (7) uses a catch-all phrase, "otherwise objectionable." This will perhaps emphasize the Ombudsman's concern with such matters as rudeness and needless delay, both of which bulk large among citizens' grievances.

(b) The Ombudsman may concern himself also with strengthening procedures and practices which lessen the risk that objectionable administrative acts will occur.

COMMENT. Subparagraph (b) makes clear that the Ombudsman should have a large and continuous interest in "preventive medicine" rather than solely in trying to abate a difficulty after it has arisen.

Section 11. *Action on complaints.* (a) The Ombudsman may receive a complaint from any source concerning an administrative act. He shall conduct a suitable investigation into the things complained of unless he believes that

1. the complainant has available to him another remedy or channel of complaint which he could reasonably be expected to use;

2. the grievance pertains to a matter outside the Ombudsman's power;

3. the complainant's interest is insufficiently related to the subject matter;

4. the complaint is trivial, frivolous, vexatious, or not made in good faith;

5. other complaints are more worthy of attention;

6. the Ombudsman's resources are insufficient for adequate investigation; or

7. the complaint has been too long delayed to justify present examination of its merit.

The Ombudsman's declining to investigate a complaint shall not, however, bar him from proceeding on his own motion to inquire into the matter complained about or into related problems;

COMMENT. The duty to act on every complaint should not be imposed, partly because the dimensions of the work burden cannot be exactly predicted and partly because some complaints will show on their face that they are unlikely to lead to productive findings. The above listing leaves the Ombudsman free to reject complaints, but does not bar his making inquiries. Specifically, he need not reject a complaint because another judicial or administrative remedy exists. Normally, one may suppose, the Ombudsman will insist that matters proceed through regular channels. Explaining to a complainant the steps he can take to obtain review will usually suffice. But assuredly some cases will arise in which the burdens of expense and time are realistic barriers to a complainant's pursuing the theoretically available remedies. In those instances access to the Ombudsman should not be precluded. Subsection (1) leaves the avenue open, but the traffic is still subject to control.

Another policy choice is reflected in Subsection (3) which does not require that every complaint be based on a claimed invasion of a strictly personal interest. This permits a complainant to bring to the Ombudsman's notice a matter of public rather than purely private concern. But if the complainant's concern with the subject matter is too attenuated, the Ombudsman may choose not to investigate.

Subsection (7) does not contain an explicit "statute of limitations" on complaints, though the Ombudsman is left free to reject those based on stale claims or ancient grudges. In Sweden complaints must be acted on if filed within ten years of the events in question; Denmark, New Zealand, and Norway, by contrast, require rejection of any complaint pertaining to occurrences beyond the preceding twelve months. Neither extreme seems desirable. The present draft lays down no rule in this respect, but allows the Ombudsman to pick his way at the outset. Later, in the light of experience, he may wish to promulgate some rules of his own, as is allowed by Section 9 (b), above.

(b) After completing his consideration of a complaint (whether or not it has been investigated) the Ombudsman shall suitably inform the complainant and, when appropriate, the administrative agency or agencies involved.

COMMENT. A decision not to investigate a complaint does not mean that it has been altogether ignored. For example, the Ombudsman and the agency involved may regard the complaint as an adequate equivalent of a petition for administrative review of which the complainant has not yet availed himself; the Ombudsman may in such a case simply forward the complaint to the appropriate appellate authority, advising the complainant that this has been done in his behalf. In other instances very extensive legal analysis may be undertaken preliminarily, leading to the conclusion that no grievance could be found to exist. In such a case the Ombudsman may be expected to write an explanatory opinion that, if foreign experience is duplicated in this country, will in the generality of instances prove wholly persuasive to the complainant. Flatly requiring the Ombudsman to state reasons whenever he decides not to investigate should, however, be avoided. Numerous complaints show on their face that they are psychopathic rather than governmental in nature. The Ombudsman's judgment must be relied upon to determine the suitable response in those instances. All practicing Ombudsmen do in fact take great pains to communicate fully and frankly with complainants, in general. This is particularly true as to cases whose merits have been explored. The Ombudsman's findings and reasoning have powerfully shaped public opinion as well as official attitudes. Conclusions adverse to a complainant's position deserve to be well explained, as has been done consistently by all foreign Ombudsmen.

Some proposals have explicitly required that if a complaint has reached the Ombudsman through a member of the legislature, the Ombudsman must report his findings and recommendations (if any) to the legislator who had forwarded his constituent's complaint. Undoubtedly the Ombudsman, guided by ordinary tact and prudence, would routinely furnish to legislative intermediaries copies of his explanations to complainants and affected officials; making statutory provision for simple courtesy seems unnecessary. If anything more is intended by the suggested requirement that the Ombudsman "report" to a legislator who has forwarded a constituent's complaint, the requirement should be resisted. The Ombudsman should not be perceived as a staff aide whose activities may be directed by individual legislators, to whom he must then report back.

(c) A letter to the Ombudsman from a person in a place of detention or in a hospital or other institution under the control of an administrative agency shall be immediately forwarded, unopened, to the Ombudsman.

COMMENT. A provision of this nature has commonly been included in ombudsman statutes. It provides a measure of psychological assurance that everyone may have ready access to the Ombudsman without fear of reprisal.

Section 12. *Consultation with agency.* Before announcing a conclusion or recommendation that criticizes an administrative agency or any person, the Ombudsman shall consult with that agency or person.

COMMENT. No provision need be made for giving specific notice that the Ombudsman has decided to investigate, if he does so decide. He will inescapably be in communication with the administrative agency when he needs its information or opinions. Formalities should be avoided lest a small organization be overborne by essentially ceremonial requirements.

At the point of announcing his conclusions, however, the Ombudsman should guard against his own mistakes by consulting those whom his findings may hurt. The requirement that he consult will not substantially impede his work, but will be a protection for all concerned against unwitting errors in fact, judgment, or expression.

Section 13. *Recommendations.* (a) If, having considered a complaint and whatever material he deems pertinent, the Ombudsman is of the opinion that an administrative agency should 1) consider the matter further, 2) modify or cancel an administrative act, 3) alter a regulation or ruling, 4) explain more fully the administrative act in question, or 5) take any other step, he shall state his recommendations to the administrative agency. If the Ombudsman so requests, the agency shall, within the time he has specified, inform him about the action taken on his recommendations or the reasons for not complying with them;

> COMMENT. Though the Ombudsman will rarely have reason to make a recommendation if he does not find an error in what the administrative agency has done or neglected to do, he should remain free to suggest improvements in method or policy even when the existing practice may be legally permissible. Thus he may facilitate one agency's learning about and taking advantage of the experience of another.

> Section 13 (a) contemplates no entry of judgment, as it were, but simply the expression of opinion by the Ombudsman. He is not a superior official, in a position of command. He cannot compel a change in an administrative act. His recommendation may, however, induce an agency to exercise whatever power it may still possess to right what the Ombudsman points out as a past mistake. Bearing in mind that consultation under Section 12 will precede recommendation under Section 13, one may safely predict that rashly critical opinions will not be expressed.

(b) If the Ombudsman believes that an administrative action has been dictated by laws whose results are unfair or otherwise objectionable, he shall bring to the .... [name of legislative body]'s notice his views concerning desirable statutory change.

> COMMENT. This subsection makes clear that the Ombudsman's duty extends beyond simply finding that an administrator acted in accord with existing statutory law; if the law itself produces unjust results, he should bring this to legislative notice. He is not meant to be a general social reformer, but he does have an obligation to take

note of statutory provisions that cause unexpectedly harsh administration.

Section 14. *Publication of recommendations.* The Ombudsman may publish his conclusions, recommendations, and suggestions by transmitting them to the .... [title of chief executive], the .... [name of legislative body] or any of its committees, the press, and others who may be concerned. When publishing an opinion adverse to an administrative agency or official he shall (unless excused by the agency or official affected) include the substance of any statement the administrative agency or official may have made to him by way of explaining past difficulties or present rejection of the Ombudsman's proposals.

> COMMENT. Bringing his views into the open is the Ombudsman's sole means of gaining the public's support. This section permits publication even when an agency has accepted a recommendation. Publicity may be needed to call other administrators' attention to current developments and also to remind the public at large that the Ombudsman is functioning for the citizenry's benefit. Publicity, however, occurs at the end and not at the beginning of discussions with the agency involved. Persuasion is the chief instrument in gaining administrative agencies' favorable response to suggestions. Only when persuasion fails will the Ombudsman begin to think about mobilizing the force of public opinion. To guard against one-sidedness, the Ombudsman is required to disclose the criticized agency's or official's view of the matter along with his own, when the two views differ.

Section 15. *Reports.* In addition to whatever reports he may make from time to time, the Ombudsman shall on or about February 15 of each year report to the .... [name of legislative body] and to the .... [title of the chief executive] concerning the exercise of his functions during the preceding calendar year. In discussing matters with which he has dealt, the Ombudsman need not identify those immediately concerned if to do so would cause needless hardship. So far as the annual report may criticize named agencies or officials, it must also include the substance of their replies to the criticism.

Section 16. *Disciplinary action against public personnel.* If the Ombudsman has reason to believe that any public official, employee, or other person has acted in a manner warranting criminal or disciplinary proceedings, he shall refer the matter to the appropriate authorities.

Section 17. *Ombudman's immunities.* (a) No proceeding, opinion, or expression of the Ombudsman shall be reviewable in any court;

COMMENT. Subsection (a) precludes judicial review of the Ombudsman's work. This preclusion simply recognizes that the Ombudsman issues no orders and takes no steps that bar anyone from pursuing preexisting remedies.

(b) No civil action shall lie against the Ombudsman or any member of his staff for anything done or said or omitted, in discharging the responsibilities contemplated by this Act;

COMMENT. Subsection (b) extends to the Ombudsman's office the immunity from harassment by lawsuit that is shared by judges and many other officials. It does not preclude criminal prosecution were serious misconduct ever to be brought to light; moreover, Section 6 provides for removal from office were the Ombudsman to be found miscreant.

(c) Neither the Ombudsman nor any member of his staff shall be required to testify or produce evidence in any judicial or administrative proceeding concerning matters within his official cognizance, except in a proceeding brought to enforce this Act.

COMMENT. Subsection (c) saves the Ombudsman's office from the awkwardness of interrupting its on-going work in order to testify about matters concerning which it may have received information (often given in confidence). The subsection does not, however, preclude the Ombudsman's testifying in proceedings needed to enforce the Act, such as an action to compel compliance with a subpoena or a prosecution against a violator under Section 19, below. The subsection does prevent his being used as an adjunct to private litigation.

Section 18. *Rights and duties of witnesses.* (a) A person required by the Ombudsman to provide information shall be paid the same fees and travel allowances as are extended to witnesses whose attendance has been required in the courts of this state;

(b) A person who, with or without service of compulsory process, provides oral or documentary information requested by the Ombudsman shall be accorded the same privileges and immunities as are extended to witnesses in the courts of this state, and shall also be entitled to be accompanied and advised by counsel while being questioned.

(c) If a person refuses to respond to the Ombudsman's subpoena, refuses to be examined, or engages in obstructive misconduct, the Ombudsman shall certify the facts to the .... [insert name of suitable court]. The court shall thereupon issue an order directing the person to appear before the court to show cause why he should not be punished as for contempt. The order and a copy of the Ombudsman's certified statement shall be served on the person.

Thereafter the court shall have jurisdiction of the matter. The same proceedings shall be had, the same penalties may be imposed, and the person charged may purge himself of the contempt in the same way as in the case of a person who has committed a contempt in the trial of a civil action before the court.

COMMENT. Subsection (c) describes the manner of enforcing subpoenas through independent judicial examination of the matter. The procedure here proposed is derived from California Government Code 11525. In all probability, the need to enforce subpoenas will not in fact arise. Information already in the possession of an administrative agency will be freely accessible to the Ombudsman. Information in a complainant's possession will of course be gladly supplied. Occasions on which data must be dragged from reluctant third parties are not likely to occur.

Section 19. *Obstruction.* A person who willfully obstructs or hinders the proper exercise of the Ombudsman's functions, or who willfully misleads or attempts to mislead the Ombudsman in his inquiries, shall be fined not more than $1,000.

COMMENT. If the enactment be by a municipality, counsel should determine whether the local legislature has power under state law to create an offence punishable by fine. Counsel must determine in each state whether necessity exists for indicating the court in which proceedings are to be brought, and upon whose initiative.

Section 20. *Relation to other laws.* The provisions of this Act are in addition to and do not in any manner limit or affect the provisions of any other enactment under which any remedy or right of appeal is provided for any person, or any procedure is provided for the inquiry into or investigation of any matter. The powers conferred on the Ombudsman may be exercised notwithstanding any provision in any enactment to the effect that any administrative action shall be final or unappealable.

Section 21. *Appropriation.* There are hereby authorized to be appropriated such sums as may be necessary to carry out the provisions of this Act.

COMMENT. The appropriations section must be shaped in accord with local practice and fiscal regulations. In some jurisdictions it need not be included in an organic statute like the one now proposed. In other jurisdictions a specific amount may have to be shown as the appropriation.

If inclusion of an appropriation section is not absolutely necessary, its omission is recommended.

Section 22. *Effective date.* This Act shall take effect immediately.

Selected Bibliography

Aaron, Richard I., "Utah Ombudsman: The American Proposals," *Utah Law Review*, No. 1 (March, 1967), pp. 32-93.

Anderman, Steven D., "The Swedish Justitieombudsman," *The American Journal of Comparative Law*, XI, No. 2 (Spring, 1962), 225-38. Reprinted in Yntema, Hessel E., ed., *The American Journal of Comparative Law Reader*. Dobbs Ferry, N.Y.: Oceana Publications, Inc., 1966, pp. 209-25.

Anderson, Stanley V., *Canadian Ombudsman Proposals*. Berkeley: Institute of Governmental Studies, 1966.

————, "Connecticut Ombudsman?" *Case and Comment*, LXX, No. 2 (March-April, 1965), 1-8.

————, "Ombudsman Proposals: Stimulus to Inquiry," *Public Affairs Report*, VII, No. 6 (December, 1966), reprinted in *Congressional Record* (January 24, 1967), pp. A238-39.

————, "The Ombudsman: Public Defender Against Maladministration," *Public Affairs Report*, VI, No. 2 (April, 1965).

————, "The Scandinavian Ombudsman," *The American-Scandinavian Review*, XII, No. 4 (December, 1964), 403-9.

Bexelius, Alfred, "The Swedish Institution of the Justitieombudsman," *International Review of Administrative Sciences*, XXVII (1961), 243-56, reprinted in *Administration* (Dublin), IX (1961-62), 272-90.

Caiden, Naomi, "An Ombudsman for Australia?" *Public Administration* (Australia), XXIII, No. 2 (June, 1964), 97-116.

————, "The Ombudsman and the Rights of the Citizen," *Australian Quarterly*, XXXVI, No. 3 (September, 1964), 69-77.

Chapman, Bruce, "The Ombudsman," *Public Administration* (London), XXXVIII, No. 4 (Winter, 1960), 303-10.

Christensen, Bent, "The Danish Ombudsman," *University of Pennsylvania Law Review*, CIX, No. 8 (June, 1961), 1100-26.

Davis, Kenneth Culp, "Ombudsmen in America: Officers to Criticize Administrative Action," *University of Pennsylvania Law Review*, CIX, No. 8 (June, 1961), 1057-76, excerpted in *Public Law* (Spring, 1962), pp. 34-42.

Farley, Marta Pisetska, and Andrew N. Farley, "An American Ombudsman: Due Process in the Administrative State," *The Administrative Law Review*, XVI (Summer, 1964), 212-21.

Frankel, Jack E., "Judicial Discipline and Removal," *Texas Law Review*, XLIV (June, 1966), 1117-35.

————, "Removal of Judges: California Tackles an Old Problem," *American Bar Association Journal*, XLIX, No. 2 (February, 1963), 166-71.

Gellhorn, Walter, *Ombudsmen and Others: Citizens' Protectors in Nine Countries.* Cambridge: Harvard University Press, 1966. Reprinted from "Citizens' Grievances Against Administrative Agencies—The Yugoslav Approach," *Michigan Law Review,* LXIV, No. 3 (January, 1966), 385-420; "Finland's Official Watchmen," *University of Pennsylvania Law Review,* CXIV, No. 3 (January, 1966), 327-64; "The Norwegian Ombudsman," *Stanford Law Review,* XVIII (January, 1966), 293-321; "The Ombudsman in Denmark," *McGill Law Journal,* XII, No. 1 (1966), 1-40; "The Ombudsman in New Zealand," *California Law Review,* LIII, No. 5 (December, 1965), 1155-1211; "Protecting Citizens Against Administrators in Poland," *Columbia Law Review,* LXV (November, 1965), 1133-66; "Review of Administrative Acts in the Soviet Union," *Columbia Law Review,* LXVI (June, 1966), 1051-79; "Settling Disagreements with Officials in Japan," *Harvard Law Review,* LXXIX, No. 4 (February, 1966), 685-732.

————, *When Americans Complain: Governmental Grievance Procedures.* Cambridge: Harvard University Press, 1966.

Hurwitz, Stephan, "Denmark's Ombudsmand: The Parliamentary Commissioner for Civil and Military Government Administration," *Wisconsin Law Review,* No. 2 (March, 1961), pp. 169-99. Reprinted as *The Ombudsman.* Copenhagen: Det danske Selskab, 1961.

Jägerskiöld, Stig, "The Swedish Ombudsman," *University of Pennsylvania Law Review,* CIX, No. 8 (June, 1961), 1077-99.

Nader, Ralph, "An Answer to Administrative Abuse," *Harvard Law Record* (December 20, 1962), pp. 13, 15.

Newman, Frank C., "Ombudsmen and Human Rights: The New U.N. Treaty Proposals," *The University of Chicago Law Review,* XXXIV, No. 4 (Summer, 1967), 951-62.

"The Ombudsman: A Symposium," *The Administrative Law Review,* XIX, No. 1 (November, 1966), 6-106.

Powles, Sir Guy, "The Citizen's Rights Against the Modern State, and Its Responsibilities to Him," *The International and Comparative Law Quarterly,* Ser. 4, Part 3, XIII (July, 1964), 761-97, and *Public Administration* (Australia), XXIII (1964), 42-68.

Reuss, Henry S., "An 'Ombudsman' for America," *New York Times Magazine* (September 13, 1964), pp. 30, 134-35.

————, and Stanley V. Anderson, "The Ombudsman: Tribune of the People," *Annals of the American Academy of Political and Social Science,* CCCLXIII (January, 1966), 44-51. Reprinted in *Congressional Record* (February 17, 1966), pp. A835-37.

————, "A Trouble-Shooter for Congress," *The Progressive,* XXX, No. 2 (February, 1966), 23-25.

Rowat, Donald C., "Finland's Defenders of the Law," *Canadian Public Administration,* IV (1960), 316-25, 412-15.

————, ed., *The Ombudsman: Citizen's Defender.* Toronto: University of Toronto Press, 1965.

————, "Ombudsmen for North America," *Public Administration Review,* XXIV, No. 4 (December, 1964), 230-33.

————, "An Ombudsman Scheme for Canada," *Canadian Journal of Economics and Political Science,* XXVIII, No. 4 (November, 1962), 543-56. Shortened and revised in *International Review of Administrative Sciences,* XXVIII, No. 4 (1962), 399-405. Reprinted in Macridis, Roy C., and Bernard E. Brown, eds., *Comparative Politics* (rev. ed.). Homewood, Ill.: Dorsey Press, Inc., 1964, pp. 470-79.

Sawer, Geoffrey, *Ombudsmen.* Melbourne: Melbourne University Press, 1964.

Secher, H. P., "Controlling the New German Military Elite: The Political Role of the Parliamentary Defense Commissioner in the Federal Republic," *Proceedings of the American Philosophical Society,* CIX (April, 1965), 63-84.

Whyatt, Sir John, ed., *The Citizen and the Administration: The Redress of Grievances.* London: Justice—British Section of the International Commission of Jurists, 1961.

Index

The American Assembly holds meetings of national leaders and publishes books to illuminate issues of United States policy. The Assembly is a national, non-partisan educational institution, incorporated in the State of New York.

The Trustees of the Assembly approve a topic for presentation in a background book, authoritatively designed and written to aid deliberations at national Assembly sessions at Arden House, the Harriman (N.Y.) Campus of Columbia University. These books are also used to support discussion at regional Assembly sessions and to evoke considerations by the general public.

All sessions of the Assembly, whether international, national, or local, issue and publicize independent reports of conclusions and recommendations on the topic at hand. Participants in these sessions constitute a wide range of experience and competence.

American Assembly books are purchased and put to use by thousands of individuals, libraries, businesses, public agencies, nongovernmental organizations, educational institutions, discussion meetings, and service groups.

The subjects of Assembly studies to date are:

1951——United States–Western Europe Relationships
1952——Inflation
1953——Economic Security for Americans
1954——The United States Stake in the United Nations
——The Federal Government Service
1955——United States Agriculture
——The Forty-Eight States
1956——The Representation of the United States Abroad
——The United States and the Far East
1957——International Stability and Progress
——Atoms for Power
1958——The United States and Africa
——United States Monetary Policy
1959——Wages, Prices, Profits, and Productivity
——The United States and Latin America
1960——The Federal Government and Higher Education
——The Secretary of State
——Goals for Americans
1961——Arms Control: Issues for the Public
——Outer Space: Prospects for Man and Society
1962——Automation and Technological Change
——Cultural Affairs and Foreign Relations
1963——The Population Dilemma
——The United States and the Middle East
1964——The United States and Canada
——The Congress and America's Future
1965——The Courts, the Public and the Law Explosion
——The United States and Japan
1966——The United States and the Philippines